A WORLD IN FLAMES
AT SEA

Peter Hepplewhite is an escaped history teacher, currently hiding in the Tyne and Wear Archives Service where he works as Education Officer. He has been a freelance writer for more than ten years, starting with school textbooks (boo!) before he realized that war stories were more thrilling.

A WORLD IN FLAMES
AT SEA

PETER HEPPLEWHITE

Illustrations and maps by David Wyatt

MACMILLAN CHILDREN'S BOOKS

To Joe, the nautical toddler

First published 2001 by Macmillan Children's Books
This edition produced 2002 by The Book People Ltd,
Hall Wood Avenue, Haydock, St Helens WA11 0UL

ISBN 0 330 48295 5

3 5 7 9 8 6 4 2

A CIP catalogue record for this book is available from the British Library.

Printed by Mackays of Chatham plc, Chatham, Kent.

CONTENTS

INTRODUCTION

In 1939 the Royal Navy was the largest naval force in the world, but it was also the most over-stretched. Britain's power depended upon trade and her vast world-wide empire – and she had 90,000 miles of ocean routes to protect. During the worst months of the war the Navy had to take on three enemies at the same time: Germany in the North Atlantic; Italy in the Mediterranean and Japan in the Far East.

Worse, the Royal Navy believed that the war at sea would be won by battleships. However, times had changed. Capital ships, like the German *Bismarck*, were a great threat but enemy submarines and aircraft proved much deadlier. It was to take the Navy years to recover from the shock, learn new lessons and hit back. But one thing was never in doubt – the courage and determination of the 'Senior Service' to fight hard – whatever the odds.

This book snapshots six stunning stories from that whirlwind time and gives you the fighting facts behind them.

• On Bonfire Night 1940, convoy HX 84 is attacked by the German pocket-battleship *Admiral Scheer*. Can the liner *Jervis Bay* buy enough time to save the convoy?

• A week later, in the Mediterranean, the Fleet Air Arm pounce on three Italian battleships in Taranto Harbour. But will 21 dated Swordfish dive-bombers be up to the job?

• The fearsome battleship, the *Bismarck*, slips out of the Baltic in May 1941. Can the Royal Navy catch her before she escapes to ravage British convoys?

• While the drama of the *Bismarck* is unfolding, Convoy OB 318 is attacked by the German submarine *U-110*. The escorts fight back, but can they go a step further and capture her precious code books?

• In August 1942 Canadian troops lead an assault on the town of Dieppe. When it all goes horribly wrong can the Navy get them home?

• In the autumn of 1943, as cold winds begin to bite in the Arctic circle, the new British secret weapon, the X-craft, strike. But will they be able to cripple the *Tirpitz*, the German ship known as 'the beast'?

A Knotty Problem

The speed of ships is measured in knots. A knot is a nautical mile. This table, based on key ships and incidents in this book, will keep you on track.

One nautical mile per hour = 1.85 kph or 1.15 mph

8–9 knots – typical speed of a convoy
= 15/16.5 kph or 9/10 mph

15 knots – the top speed of the *Jervis Bay*, as she dashed head-on towards the *Scheer*
= 27 kph or 17 mph

16.5 knots – the top speed of a **corvette**
= 31 kph or 19 mph

17.5 knots – the top speed of a Type VII U-boat on the surface
= 32 kph or 20 mph

291/2 knots – the top speed of the *Mighty Hood*
= 55 kph or 34 mph

70 knots – the take-off speed of a Swordfish torpedo bomber from an aircraft carrier
= 130 kph or 80 mph

THE HEROES OF CONVOY HX 84

BATTLE BRIEFING

The Battle of the Atlantic

Only one battle was fought both night and day throughout the whole of World War II – the Battle of the Atlantic. Ships were Britain's lifeblood. To keep on fighting, a vast range of supplies was needed every month – everything from potatoes to petrol. In 1940 alone, 41 million tons of cargo were unloaded in UK ports. Most came across the Atlantic from the USA and Canada. If the German Navy, the **Kriegsmarine**, *could sink enough vessels Britain would grind to a halt and her people starve.*

This put Britain's merchant (civilian) seamen in the front line. The men who sailed under the 'Red Duster', the flag of the merchant navy, risked death by mine, bomb, shell or torpedo every time they put to sea. When the war ended in August 1945, at least 45,000 seamen had been listed as killed, wounded or missing.

4

The Royal Navy quickly relearned hard lessons from World War I. Most ships were ordered to sail in convoys, protected by armed escorts – destroyers, corvettes and emergency vessels like trawlers and cargo ships hastily armed with guns. Even so, they were highly vulnerable to attack. By the winter of 1940 losses mounted and it seemed Nazi Germany was winning!

Surface Raiders

Erich Raeder, Commander in Chief of the Kriegsmarine (the German navy), fought a cunning war. He knew his forces couldn't take on the Royal Navy in a head-on fight. The German surface fleet (ships, not submarines) was far too small. Instead he used his bigger warships in a campaign of hit and run raids on British convoys. This reached its peak between November 1940 and March 1941. During these grim winter months, the battleships Scharnhorst, Gneisenau and the **pocket battleship** Admiral Scheer ravaged the Atlantic convoys.

The Admiral Scheer

Most sailors think of their ships as women or girls. They lovingly call them 'she' or 'her', even when they have macho names like Warspite or Victory. Yet, for the German Kriegsmarine, the Admiral Scheer was different. Launched in 1933, this sleek pocket battleship had a sense of raw power. When the crew talked respectfully about their ship, it was always as a male – 'der' Scheer.

A scene from the launch celebrations
of the *Admiral Scheer*, 1933.

On 23 October 1940 the *Admiral Scheer* slipped quietly to sea from Gotenhaven in the Baltic. Captain Theodore Krancke was in command. His mission was to seek and destroy British convoys – without putting his ship at risk. The more helpless the targets the better. This was war at its cruellest.

The *Scheer* was the perfect raider. 'He' had a top speed of 26 knots and a main armament of six 11-inch (280mm) guns – sufficient to outrun or outgun most Royal Navy warships. And with full tanks, 'his' frugal diesel engines gave a range of over 20,000 miles (30,000 km) at a cruising speed of 15 knots (27 kph). Fate too was on the *Scheer*'s side. Using radar to avoid unidentified ships, Krancke dodged the Royal Navy and slipped into the North Atlantic undetected. Even the weather helped. A ferocious storm washed two men overboard, but kept enemy reconnaissance (spotter) planes on the ground. A tiger was on the loose – and the British knew nothing about it!

A Nazi propaganda shot. A view along the *Scheer's* deck to the formidable 11-inch guns, c. 1936.

Within a few days Krancke caught the scent of a victim. The German radio interception service, the 'B' service, informed him that Convoy HX 84 had left Halifax in Canada on 28 October. Allowing for the slow speed of a gaggle of merchant ships – only 8–9 knots – Krancke believed that the enemy should be close by.

On the morning of 5 November, he launched one of the *Scheer*'s tiny Arada seaplanes. At noon the pilot, Lieutenant Pietsch, returned safely and reported HX 84 was within striking distance, to the south. And better still, the merchant ships had no Royal Navy escorts. Krancke decided to attack at once. With luck he would come within range before the British realized it was a German battleship bearing down on them.

The Jervis Bay

There were 38 ships in convoy HX 84, carrying vital supplies to Britain – gasoline, kerosene, fuel oil, steel, pit props, scrap iron, trucks, newsprint, wool and maize. But Pietsch had made a mistake. They *were* protected by a single escort, an Armed Merchant Cruiser (AMC) – a fast cargo-liner hastily equipped with old guns when war broke out. She was the *Jervis Bay* and her captain was 48-year-old Edward Fogarty Fegan.

The *Jervis Bay* was the least formidable of convoy escorts. She offered some protection against a U-boat on the surface, but not much else. Even if Theodore

The *Jervis Bay.*

Krancke had known she was there, he wouldn't have altered his plans.

A little before 16:00 hours a lone warship was seen approaching HX 84 at high speed. Fegan was puzzled. He wasn't expecting any other escorts, but she would certainly be useful. The gun crews could see the silhouette of the mystery ship clearly through their sights. Their best guess was an 'R' class battleship. An impressive friend! Quartermaster Sam Patience wasn't so sure. He didn't like the look of the peculiar 'tiddly top' on the funnel. It didn't seem quite right – not British.

'Find out who she is,' Fegan ordered.

The chief yeoman signalled with the Aldis lamp: 'What ship?'

And again: 'What ship? What ship?'

But there was no answering flash in the evening gloom.

'Stubborn set of blokes on that bridge,' mused Fegan, beginning to fear the worst.

A few minutes later, any lingering hopes faded. It was clear the mystery ship was a large enemy warship. Fegan cursed quietly to himself. All the German battleships were supposed to be bottled up in the Baltic! It was a terrible shock, but almost at once he decided to fight.

In a flurry of activity, red rockets lit up the winter gloom – the emergency signal for the convoy to scatter. More than a few sailors watched the flares with heavy hearts. It was Guy Fawkes Night, but these were fireworks they could have done without. Then, as if adding to the mood of a mad bonfire night party, the crew of the *Jervis Bay* hurled dustbin-sized smoke floats over the side. Soon there was a wall of smoke between the convoy and the *Scheer*, giving the ships of HX 84 some cover. This done, Fegan ordered full steam ahead and at a speed of 15 knots steered straight for the enemy.

To attack a battleship wasn't foolish heroics. Fegan was the fifth generation of his family to serve in the Navy and he knew exactly what he was doing. The *Jervis Bay* was bait to draw the enemy's fire. He was going to sacrifice his ship and crew to give the others a chance. And every second gained was vital. Night was falling and darkness offered protection – if he could keep the *Scheer* busy!

It was a brave but forlorn battle. At 17:10, with the range down to 17 kilometres, the *Scheer* turned broadside on and opened a ferocious barrage. Every turret was directed at the AMC – and for the German gunners it was like shooting ducks in a barrel. The tall liner was an easy target and her seven old guns completely outranged.

The first German salvo wrecked the bridge and the radio room, severely wounding Fegan. The huge ship bucked and rolled as the shells slammed home. The third salvo caught the *Jervis Bay* amidships, smashing the deck superstructure. Soon she was ablaze, her guns knocked out and many of the crew dead. Some, their clothes on fire, threw themselves over the side, choosing to drown rather than burn. The last time Sam saw Captain Fegan, the gallant officer was standing grimly by the wheel, one of his arms partly severed.

For 22 long minutes the *Jervis Bay* charged towards the *Scheer*, reeling under blast after blast. By rights she should have sunk quickly but the British had learned a sharp lesson early in the war. AMCs were not designed to take shell fire and several had gone down so fast that their crews hadn't been able to escape. Now they sailed with their holds full of empty barrels, for extra buoyancy. It was the barrels that gave the *Jervis Bay* an edge. Battered and broken, she still stayed afloat.

This seemed to trouble Krancke. Long after the AMC was a wreck, the merciless bombardment went on. Finally, soon after 17:30, the *Jervis Bay* keeled over. With supreme courage she had got to within a mile of the *Scheer*.

Captain Fegan went down with his ship and was

The *Scheer* attacking the *Jervis Bay*.

awarded a posthumous VC. Yet he and almost 200 crew-men did not die in vain. The time they had bought saved countless other lives. Daylight had almost gone before Krancke turned away to look for new victims and most of convoy HX 84 had slipped away. That evening the *Scheer* hunted down and sank six ships, a total of 38,720 tons. It was bad, but without Fegan's hard-nosed guts, the massacre would have been far worse.

Cheating Death
For the few survivors of the *Jervis Bay* the agony went on. When the order to abandon ship came, Sam Patience

had a problem. Like a lot of sailors, he couldn't swim! Sam thought, 'Well, I've got to make a decision here. Either I die with the ship or get over the side.'

He decided to risk the sea, pulling a lifebelt from its shattered casing. But even getting off the AMC was a nightmare. Sam pulled the lifebelt over his head and slid 40 feet (15 m) down what he thought was a rope. It wasn't. It was a steel hawser (cable) and tore his hands to the bone.

For an hour and a half Sam floated in the freezing waves. Each time he topped a crest he saw distant gun flashes – the *Scheer* doing its grisly work. Just as he was giving up hope, fate flicked a coin and came down in Sam's favour. A lifeboat appeared, one of the *Jervis Bay*'s own boats that had not been smashed. He was hauled aboard but the outlook wasn't good – a handful of injured and shocked men in an open boat. Sam reckoned that at best he had swapped a quick death for a slow one. Yet determinedly, they took turns using a small torch to flash out SOS into the empty ocean.

Two hours later a vessel hove into view. At first, the sailors took it for a German prison ship, mopping up after the *Scheer*. They could even hear foreign voices shouting in the distance. It was shattering, but better a prisoner than dead. Then a clear Scottish voice rang out: 'You're all right now, lads!'

Laughing with relief, Sam saw their rescuer was one of the convoy, the Swedish *Stureholm*. Her captain, Sven

Olander, had reckoned she was too slow to risk outrunning the *Scheer*. Instead he'd played a clever game. The *Stureholm* had stopped her engines and stayed put in the smoke screen laid by the *Jervis Bay*. Four hours later Olander had crept out of cover and saw a lonely torch signalling in the distance. Olander brought his Scottish stoker on deck to talk to any survivors.

All his life Sam remembered the kindness of the Swedish crew. 'They carried us up to the officer's quarters and they laid us on the deck. Filled us with a tot of vodka or rum and they put raw iodine on my hands.' He was safe.

A Floating Bomb

As Sam Patience took his well-earned rest, others were still fighting for their lives. One of the next targets to attract the attention of the *Scheer* was the tanker *San Demetrio*. She was carrying 12,000 tonnes of aviation fuel and her Master, Captain George Waite, was only too aware that a single hit could turn her into an inferno.

Although he tried to run, the tanker was soon caught, silhouetted against the moon. As the first salvo burst nearby, Waite gave the order to 'abandon ship'. It was not a moment too soon. As the crew lowered the lifeboats, shells crashed into the bow and the bridge. They had barely time to move off before the whole of the aft and midships sections burst into flames.

The men realized that their ship was a floating bomb. If she blew up, burning fuel would spew on to the sea and roast them alive.

'Put your backs into it, boys,' roared Mr Hawkins, the Second Officer, 'let's get to windward of her. If she goes we don't stand a chance.'

The *Scheer* started shelling again and tracer bullets ripped across the surface of the sea like glowing cigarette butts. To add to the sailors' misery, the wind strengthened to gale force – a storm was brewing. Spray washed over them and within minutes everyone was soaked to the skin. It was going to be a long night.

Rescue – for Some

Of the three lifeboats that escaped, two, including Captain Waite's, were rescued by the *City of Gloucester*. The *Gloucester* had fallen behind her own convoy when she picked up a distress call from HX 84. Regardless of the danger, her Master, Captain Smith, changed course to look for survivors. He took a gamble that the *Scheer* would not hang around in case the Royal Navy showed up. He was right, but who was to know if U-boats were lurking? During a risky search, he rescued most of the *San Demetrio* men and survivors from seven other boats and rafts – a total of 92 snatched from a lingering death.

The third lifeboat from the tanker, with Chief Engineer Pollard in charge, was the most crowded.

Sixteen sailors packed its tiny thwartes (seats). Around noon on 6 November, they spotted a ship, probably the *Gloucester*. Desperately they fired flares to show their position, but horror of horrors it sailed on. The disappointment hit them like a blow in the stomach. Spirits sagged. They were cold, exhausted, frightened. And about to begin an amazing adventure.

That afternoon a blazing hulk drifted into view on the horizon. As they rowed closer they were stunned to see that it was their own ship. The *San Demetrio* was still afloat! With no chance of rescue they decided to reboard her and see what could be done. But what a choice – drift in the Atlantic until you die or try to save a burning oil tanker. Able Seaman Calum MacNeil remembered: 'She was the only thing we could see in the whole wide circle of ocean, and she looked good.'

The Ship That Wouldn't Die

The *San Demetrio* was in a dire mess. Fire had destroyed the crew's quarters and the bridge. The engine room was flooded. The wireless, compasses, steering gear and charts had all been destroyed. The deck plates were crumpled like cardboard and riddled with shell holes. Every time the ship rolled, petrol spouted out of the tanks and flowed past smouldering debris. It was little short of a miracle that she hadn't exploded.

Over the next 48 hours the scratch crew rose to the challenge. First they formed a bucket party and began to tackle the worst fires. While this backbreaking work was underway the engineers rebuilt an electric generator to pump fuel to the boilers. This was a crucial step. Once the boilers were steamed up they had power! Power for hoses to fight the flames. And power to get the ship underway. Next they plugged the holes in the deck with thick cotton wadding and finally, by about 14:00 on 8 November, the steering gear had been repaired. With the engines running sweetly at 90 revs per minute, the *San Demetrio* set sail for England.

But how to find home without any navigation aids? Here skills as old as time came into play. They kept to an easterly course, guided by the Pole Star at night and the sun at dawn.

And how to keep the crew fed when most of the food had been destroyed? They lived on a plain but nourishing diet of potatoes and onions cooked in a pail with steam from the boilers.

And how to tend their many injuries? They doctored one another. When Pollard's finger swelled to several times its normal size, a shipmate plunged a penknife through his nail. This released a fountain of pus and probably saved him from blood poisoning.

At last, on Wednesday 13 November, the *San Demetrio* put into Blacksod Bay in Ireland. She had made it against the odds and her weary crew became national heroes. Convoy HX 84 had been on a journey to hell and back again.

FIGHTING FACTS

Saved by a Banana Boat

At 14:30 on 5 November, as the *Scheer* raced towards HX 84, the Germans spotted a single merchant ship. It was the *Mopan*, a banana boat, making her way alone from Kingston, Jamaica to Britain. If she sent out SOS signals by radio the convoy would be warned and scatter. Since the *Scheer* could not slip past her unseen, Captain Krancke knew he had to deal with this nuisance quickly. He sped towards the ship and fired a warning shell at close range. The stunned crew were ordered to abandon ship and, faced with a battery of 11-inch (280 mm) guns, not surprisingly obeyed.

They did not risk sending a warning first, but even so they unwittingly helped to save HX 84. It took the *Scheer* an hour to take the *Mopan*'s men prisoner and sink the banana boat with a salvo of 10.5cm shells below the waterline. Crucially, it was already dusk by the time Krancke reached his target.

No Survivors

Another victim of the *Scheer* was the 10,042-ton *Beaverford*. She was caught soon after dark, carrying ammunition, timber and food. Like the *Jervis Bay* she tried to buy time for the others and opened up with two tiny guns. It was like tackling a lion with a fly-swatter. Hit by twelve rounds from the battleship's big guns, she burst into flames and exploded. Krancke finished her off with a torpedo. The *Beaverford* sank with all hands on board – 77 courageous officers and men.

Hopeless Odds

Captain Fegan won the Victoria Cross 'for valour in challenging hopeless odds and giving his life to save the many ships it was his duty to protect'. When medals were given the details of the awards were published in the *London Gazette*. Unusually the *Gazette* added: 'Among those who went down in the *Jervis Bay* there must have been many, and among the survivors others, whose gallantry, were the whole truth known, also deserved decoration.'

It was a way of saying the whole crew had been heroes.

Liberty Ships

When the war began the British merchant navy was the biggest in the world – 27 per cent of world tonnage, a fleet of 6,843 vessels. But even so, by the end of 1940 there was a crisis. The Germans were sinking Allied ships faster than they could be replaced. The answer was American know-how.

The dynamic industrialist Henry J. Kaiser began to build ships in a completely new way. His Baltimore shipyards mass-produced hundreds of identical cargo vessels. They were based on a design supplied by a British company, J. L. Thompson's of Sunderland, and boldly called 'Liberty Ships'.

Traditionally ships were built and fitted out by hundreds of craftsmen, almost as if they were medieval cathedrals. In the Kaiser yards prefabricated sections were delivered from factories and welded together on the slipways by semi-skilled workers, including women. The first American Liberty Ship, the *SS Patrick Henry*, was launched on 27 September 1941. She took 240 days to build, but soon this time was cut to 42 days per vessel. A record was set when the *Robert E. Peary* was built, from laying the keel to delivery, in eight days. In 1942 597 Liberty Ships were launched in the USA and this rocketed to a total of 2,710 vessels by the end of the war. Of these, 200 were sunk in action.

Scandal at Sea

Pay and conditions in the British merchant navy were often poor. An ordinary seaman might earn only £6 per month for working ten hours a day, seven days a week. There was no paid leave at the end of a voyage, no matter how long it had lasted. If a man wanted to spend time with his family he had to go off pay.

Worse, under British law when a ship was sunk a sailor's wage stopped. Think about it! A survivor from a torpedoed ship was unemployed and unpaid as soon as his vessel sank beneath the waves! Some of the more responsible shipping companies paid rescued men – but some didn't! When they got back to Britain all they were given was a free train ticket and 2/6d (12½p) to help them get home. Some reward!

The Secret Raiders

Remembering German successes during World War I, Admiral Raeder attacked Allied shipping with a fleet of nine secret raiders. These were a mixed bag of converted merchant ships packed with guns and torpedo tubes. One trick was to change their appearance with dummy funnels and decks. Often the raiders got close to their victims by disguising themselves as British ships. Foiled by their hit and run tactics, it took the Royal Navy many months to hunt them down.

The German ship *Atlantis* began a round the world – 176,000 km – voyage of destruction in March 1940. Under the command of daring Captain Rogge, she sank 22 ships before she was sent to the bottom by the cruiser *Devonshire* in the South Atlantic. Rogge and most of his crew were rescued by a U-boat.

The *Kormoran* sank eleven ships before she was cornered near Sharksbay, Australia, by the cruiser HMAS (His Majesty's Australian Ship) *Sydney*. In a gruelling battle both vessels were sunk and all 645 men aboard the *Sydney* died.

A New Enemy

If the British were suffering heavy losses in the Atlantic

in November 1940, in the Mediterranean they were about to strike back. This time the enemy was Italy . . .

OPERATION JUDGEMENT

BATTLE BRIEFING

Benito Mussolini, the leader of the Italian Fascist party, took power in 1922. He dreamed of building 'a new Roman Empire', and became an ally of Nazi Germany and Japan in 1936. Even so, Mussolini waited until France was as good as beaten before he joined in the war in June 1940. The American President Roosevelt commented bitterly, 'The hand that held the dagger (Italy) has struck it into the back of its neighbour (France).'

The Italian navy now threatened British convoys in the Mediterranean, including vital tankers bringing oil from the Persian Gulf. Worse, when France surrendered on 24 June, the French fleet seemed likely to end up in German hands. For a while, the Royal Navy considered pulling out of the 'Med' altogether. This would have meant certain defeat for the British troops in North Africa and the Middle East.

Instead, under Admiral Cunningham, the Navy reorganized and hit back. The French fleet was destroyed at anchor at its bases at Oran and Mers-El Kebirs. After this swift and ruthless action, Cunningham turned his attention to the Italians. He tried to force them into battle, but the enemy admirals were under strict orders not to risk a full-scale confrontation with the Royal Navy. On paper the Italian navy was powerful, but the crews were poorly trained and lacked confidence.

After months of shadow-boxing Cunningham dusted off a plan first made in 1935, when Mussolini had caused a crisis by invading Ethiopia. If the Italian navy would not come out and fight, he would take the war to them. Swordfish torpedo bombers were given a breath-taking mission: attack the Italian fleet at night as it lay in Taranto harbour. The idea was brilliant, but could it work? Success depended on the skill and bravery of young Fleet Air Arm (FAA) pilots like Lieutenant John Wellham. This is his story.

Judgement Day

11 November, Armistice Day. The day World War I ended in 1918. And the day millions of Europeans should have been united in remembrance, peace and sadness. But this was 1940 and Europe was at war again. In the Mediterranean, havoc was about to break out. The Royal Navy was ready to launch 'Operation Judgement' – the code name for the attack on the Italian naval base at Taranto.

As dusk fell, Lieutenant John Wellham paced the quarter deck. A pilot in the Fleet Air Arm, John was serving aboard the Navy's finest aircraft carrier, HMS *Illustrious*. As the great ship broke away from the rest of the fleet, he watched her escort of cruisers and destroyers build up speed – always an awesome sight. The sea, deep blue and calm, was sliced open by bright wakes of spray. The mighty carrier was heading for the attack position, near the Greek island of Cephalonia, 195 miles from the target. Close to the enemy, but not too close.

The waiting was always the worst. Once the final briefing was over and the aircraft checked and rechecked, time hung heavily for John. His thoughts dwelt on the fearsome mission ahead. '21 Swordfish,' he mused. 'Only 21 dated torpedo bombers to cripple a battle fleet. Have we a hope in hell?'

Naval Pilot

At school, John could never decide between joining the Navy or the RAF. He loved ships and planes, so which was it to be? Pity it couldn't be both. In the end the RAF made him an offer he couldn't refuse: a short service commission, only four years. If he didn't like it, he wouldn't be too old to start over at something else.

John joined up, aged 17, in 1936 and earned his 'Wings' in 1937. He served for a year in a light bomber squadron and survived a crash-landing which left the ASI (air speed indicator, like the speedometer in a car) stuck at 180 mph (290 kph) – the impact speed of the plane!

John gained a new companion from this lucky escape. His injuries were so light he reckoned a guardian angel must have helped him out. He was to rely on his help over and over again in the coming years.

In spite of a broken leg and severe bruises John still enjoyed the RAF, until he saw an Air Ministry notice. The Navy had taken control of the Fleet Air Arm from the Royal Air Force and wanted to recruit pilots. Those who 'came aboard' were offered Navy commissions (they were made officers). It was the perfect answer to his boyhood dilemma – a flyer on a ship.

When John was appointed to the torpedo training Unit at Gosport, he saw the Fairey Swordfish plane for the first time. It was not a pretty sight.

We looked at it with awe and one wag asked, 'Does it fly?' No artist would have dashed off to get his sketch pad. It looked as if the various parts had been added as afterthoughts.

The Swordfish torpedo bomber was the backbone of the Fleet Air Arm but in 1939 it was already old-fashioned – a biplane with an open cockpit and a top speed of only 140 mph (225 kph). It looked like a mis-placed relic from World War I.

Yet in weeks of intense training John learned why the Navy loved the plane nicknamed the 'Stringbag'. It proved to be robust, forgiving and almost impossible to stall, and the Bristol Pegasus engine was totally reliable.

The Fairey Swordfish torpedo bomber.

A very comforting thought in long flights over rough seas. Better still, the Swordfish had a very short take-off and packed a hefty punch. With a crew of two or three, it could carry a large choice of weapons – a single 1,600 lb (725 kg) torpedo, eight 250 lb (113 kg) bombs or four depth charges. Later in the war the Swordfish was even equipped with radar and rockets.

War with Italy

John was serving with 824 Squadron, aboard the carrier *Eagle*, when the war began in September 1939. She was stationed in the Far East – out of it, as far as the real war was concerned. The *Eagle* spent months vainly hunting German surface raiders in the Indian Ocean, or escorting convoys from Australia. All the while the news from Europe grew worse.

On 10 May 1940 Hitler's troops marched into France and John's frustrating time came to an abrupt end. The *Eagle* was ordered to join the Mediterranean Fleet, based at Alexandria in Egypt. She arrived barely days before Italy declared war on 10 June. Almost at once the action began, as the Royal Navy tried to bring the Italians to battle.

The *Eagle* drew her first blood at Tobruk in Libya, when Swordfish attacked the port and sank a destroyer. A few days later, on 9 July, John was in a fierce but indecisive fight. As British and Italian warships squared up in the Gulf of Calabria, Admiral Cunningham ordered the Swordfish into action. 824 Squadron took off at midday, eager for the kill, but came back disappointed. As the Swordfish dived from 7,000 ft (2,130 m) they ran into a barrage of anti-aircraft (AA) fire. John chose his target but it proved difficult to get a clear bearing on an enemy ship dodging at high speed. He took his best shot and missed. And so did every other FAA pilot.

Score: Britain nil.

Only hours later, it was the *Eagle*'s turn to zigzag desperately while bombers from bases in Italy droned high overhead. Thankfully, they too missed.

Score: Italy nil.

No ships were sunk that July day, but military history

was made. It was the first battle at sea in which both sides used aircraft. No one realized the importance of this at the time, but it was an omen. In 1942–43 the great sea battles would be won by planes. The admirals didn't like it and many barely understood it, but the days of the battleship were over.

The Illustrious

In late August the pilots on the *Eagle* were buzzing with excitement. A spanking new aircraft carrier had arrived to join the Mediterranean fleet – HMS *Illustrious*. She was a 23,000-ton giant that left them green with envy. John chuckled when he thought of the *Eagle* – a converted battleship, based on a hull laid down before 1914. Her flight deck narrowed to a point and her bows curved forward like the ram of an ancient war galley. The *Illustrious*, however, was state of the art – fast, with an armoured deck and radar, and bristling with powerful AA guns.

The new arrival boosted the **morale** of the whole fleet and quickened the pulse of Admiral Andrew Browne Cunningham. Nicknamed 'ABC', Cunningham was commander of the Royal Navy in the 'Med' – and had a reputation as a fighter. He was itching to go after the Italians and the *Illustrious* was just the ship he needed. Overnight his air power had more than doubled. And that meant his grand-slam plan – 'Operation Judgement' – was on.

Taranto

Taranto was a major Italian naval base – the equivalent of Scapa Flow or Portsmouth in Britain. It was a magnificent harbour, tucked inside the heel on the boot shape of southern Italy. Early in November, the final piece of the jigsaw dropped into place. Reconnaissance planes spotted six battleships moored in the Mare Grande – the shallow, outer harbour. The targets were waiting.

When the aircrew were briefed John discovered how dangerous the raid would be. Taranto was strongly defended with around 300 AA guns, plus those on the ships. Backing these up were lines of **barrage balloons** – a real hazard for a low-level attack – searchlights and torpedo nets (protective nets around the battleships to

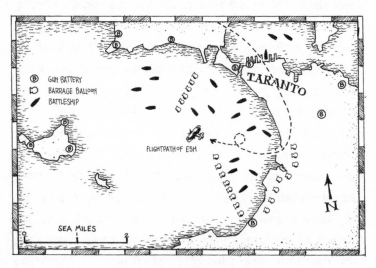

The plan for 'Operation Judgement'.

catch torpedoes). They didn't find out until later that 'ABC' expected to lose half his planes in the raid. This was considered an acceptable loss, but no one asked the pilots what they thought!

The first plan for 'Operation Judgement' was to use 30 Swordfish, hitting the base in two waves of fifteen, on 21 October – Trafalgar Day. Then the problems began.

First, the *Illustrious* had a fire in the hanger deck and the date was put back to 30 October. Next, the *Eagle* was damaged by near misses from over 300 Italian bombs in two days and sea water seeped into her aviation fuel tanks. The old warrior couldn't take her place in the attack.

Finally, five planes and eight crews were transferred from the *Eagle* to the *Illustrious*, including John. The raid was reset for the next moonlit night, 11 November.

Success now rested on just 21 Swordfish, twelve in the first wave and nine in the second. Six in each group were armed with torpedoes and the rest with bombs and flares.

Take-Off

By 19:30 on 11 November, the flight deck of the *Illustrious* was busy as an ants' nest. The planes in the first strike were ranged at the end of the deck, while the carrier brought her speed up to 30 knots (55 kph). This increased the wind force over the flight deck and helped the heavily laden aircraft take off. On the quarter deck,

Preparing the Swordfish for take-off.

near the stern, John's teeth grated as the vibration of the propellers shook the ship.

At 20:30 the first Swordfish trundled off, the others following in quick succession. John was assigned to the second wave – 45 minutes to go. Now the time that had dragged so badly seemed to rush by in a blur of activity. The planes from the second wave had been brought on deck by the time John had dressed in his flying suit. Some pilots discreetly collected their good luck charms. John contented himself with a private word with his guardian angel.

'Come on, old man. Do your stuff.'

At 21:15 he was seated in his plane, E5H, with obser-vor/navigator Pat Humphreys strapped in behind. The faithful Pegasus engine fired perfectly and the aircraft handlers performed their usual hair-raising trick, ducking round the spinning propellers to pull the chocks away. As the *Illustrious* surged up to 30 knots (55 kph) again, John scooted down the flight deck – lifting gently into the air as the air speed indicator reached 70 knots.

Once airborne they took their place in the formation and counted aircraft. There were only seven, two were missing. Later, John was told, one plane had been damaged in a collision, while the other had lost its long-range tank shortly after take-off. Knowing he wouldn't have enough fuel to reach Taranto, the pilot had turned back.

Only eight planes in the second wave, already the odds were worse. 'Let's hope,' John thought, 'that the others have had more luck.'

A little over an hour later he had his answer. The dark blue of the horizon was lit by an eerie glow. Taranto!

And the place was alive and hopping. And burning.

Tracers (brightly coloured marker shells, to help the gunners take aim) from the AA guns lit up the sky like crazy, pulsing floodlights. The first wave had certainly upset the Italian defences. They were blasting in all directions, setting up a wall of flak. Yet oddly, this awesome barrage helped. Together with the bright moonlight, the glare of the tracer showed up the harbour in brilliant detail.

'It looks just like the reconnaissance photographs,' John mumbled.

Pat chirped up from behind, speaking through the communication tubes: 'The course for the *Illustrious* should be about 135 degrees. You might like to set it now.'

He was looking after his pilot. If Pat was killed during the raid, John would know which way to head for home.

Judgement Time

The Swordfish swooped in line astern, holding a loose formation as they circled round the main harbour. One by one the planes peeled off to go after individual targets.

'Hang on, I'm going in,' John called.

'OK. Do your worst. Good luck,' came the calm reply. Pat seemed unflappable.

Down they went, picking up speed as the dive steepened . . . 140 knots . . . 150 knots . . . 170 knots. Lines of yellow, green and red tracer whipped past. They seemed to only just miss, zipping under and over the aircraft. Even the screaming slipstream stank of cordite. Still, it wasn't the AA fire that hit them . . .

'Blast! A barrage balloon,' John cursed. No time to miss . . . thwack . . . hit the cable . . . E5H juddered violently, the stick flew out of his hand.

In an instant they were plummeting, out of control towards the centre of Taranto city.

'What the . . .?' John's mind was a blur of reactions and decisions.

The wings were still there. Heave back on the stick ...
nothing ... Try again ... HEAVE ... no technique, just
brute strength.

Thank God. Some response.

He hauled the stick back into his lap. Slowly, oh so
slowly, they levelled out, barely skimming over the
houses and factory chimneys. Then out over the black
waters of the harbour.

The plane was crippled, but how badly? What next?

Ditch? No, too fast, they'd smash up in the sea. Head
for home? No! They'd carried that ruddy torpedo all this
way. Jolly well going to have a shot at something.

A fast look round. There on the horizon! The huge silhouette of a battleship, rising in a mass of decks, turrets
and bridges, like a child's castle. Pat recognized the out-
line, she was the *Vittoria Veneto*.

John swung the Swordfish in a sharp 180-degree turn
and hugged the sea, closing in on the target. Struggling to
keep the stricken aircraft level, he skidded in, giving her
left rudder and keeping the right wing down a little.

Not much flak. Wrong! They've seen us.

Suddenly the side of the battleship glowed as the
Italians opened up with everything but the 15-inch guns.
Strings of light pulsed out towards E5H – and missed.
They were aiming too high.

Don't get too close. Remember the safety range.
Now!

John hit the release button on the throttle lever and

the torpedo dropped away. With the 1,600 lb (725 kg) load gone, the plane jumped in the air. Straight into the flak.

STUUNGGG. Another hit.

'Fly!' John muttered as he fought the sloppy controls. He had to get her under the guns again before they were swatted like an annoying hornet.

And abruptly it was over. They were away, darting over the waves. Cloaked by the dark, AA fire from the *Vittoria* whipped over and past them, the tracer vanishing harmlessly into the distance.

So far, so lucky. But would the damaged plane get them home? Once clear of Taranto, John was able to assess the problems. The engine seemed fine; revs fine; oil pressure OK. The flight instruments, however, were haywire. The Swordfish was flying like a crab. Soon his left leg ached with the effort of applying left rudder to stay in a straight line.

If John had doubts about poor old E5H, he had none about Pat. The navigator's directions were quick and confident. Course given, he sat back and listened to a Verdi opera on radio Milan. You had to say one thing for the Italians, they wrote decent music. An hour later, when Pat picked up the beacon from the *Illustrious*, their heading was spot on.

One snag left – landing in the dark. John banked to the left and lost height in a wide circuit over the carrier. As he approached he dropped the arrestor hook and cut the revs. Instantly he lost control and banged open the throttle again. The DLCO (Deck Landing Control Officer) signalled furiously: 'Too fast, too fast'. But there was nothing John could do. E5H hurtled in, missed the first arrestor wires then caught with a terrific jerk. The wheels hit the deck with a satisfying thud. They were down.

FIGHTING FACTS

Taranto – Damage Assessment

It was several days before John and the other FAA pilots knew the result of their raid. It was better than they dared hope for. Three battleships had been sunk at their moorings – the *Littorio*, the *Duilio* and the *Cavour*. The *Cavour* was out of action for good and the others took months to repair. This was half the enemy battle-line. The Italian Seaplane Base at Taranto was completely destroyed and the oil depot set ablaze.

Amazingly, all except two of the Swordfish made it back safely. After this the Italian navy pulled out of Taranto to its base in Naples, out of reach of the FAA. The attack had shown, beyond doubt, that the aircraft carrier had become the most important weapon at sea.

Pearl Harbour

Admiral Yamamoto, Commander of the Japanese fleet, found the attack on Taranto extremely interesting. In a

The Italian battleship *Cavour*, which was sunk
in the attack at Taranto harbour.

locked drawer of his desk, aboard his flagship *Nagato*,
there was a 500-page book with the title *The Habits,
Strengths and Defences of the American Fleet in the
Hawaiian Area.* Japan was still at peace with the USA but
Yamamoto was planning for war. Inspired by the Royal
Navy, he realized a similar air strike against the US base

at Pearl Harbor was possible. From 12 November 1940, Operation Z, as Yamamoto called it, was given priority. Just over a year later, on Sunday, 7 December 1941, 350 Japanese aircraft bombed the American fleet in a surprise attack. As a result, America declared war on Japan and the war in the Pacific began.

Target – the Illustrious

War can be like a pendulum, swinging first one way and then another. For a brief time the attack on Taranto gave the British control of the Mediterranean, then the Luftwaffe (German air force) stepped in. In December 1940, the German High Command sent **Fliegerkorps X** to prop up the Italians. This was a crack unit specially trained to attack ships. It was equipped with 'pure' dive-bombers, the Stuka 87, and shallow dive-bombers, the twin-engined Junkers 88. The pilots had one overriding order – 'Sink the *Illustrious*.'

On 10 January the Germans sprang an ambush. Their devastating attack took only ten minutes:

12:00: The *Illustrious* was escorting a large convoy loaded with supplies for the British army in the Middle East. She carried Fulmar fighters and a patrol was airborne, on the watch for enemy raids.

12:20: A pair of Italian torpedo bombers swept in low over the sea. They loosed their weapons and sped off – with the British fighters in hot pursuit. The carrier wheeled sharply and the torpedoes passed harmlessly to either side. This attack was a ruse to draw off the Fulmars – and it had worked.

12:30: The radar screens on the *Illustrious* showed a swarm of around 40 planes closing in from the north at 12,000 ft (3655 m). A second flight of Fulmars was preparing to take off. They struggled into the air but couldn't gain the height needed to break up the German assault.

12:35: Peeling off in flights of three, the dive-bombers swooped down on the *Illustrious*. The Stukas dropped to point-blank range. They were so low that as they pulled out of their dives, they shot across the flight deck below the level of the carrier's funnel. The *Illustrious* weaved and threw up a mass of AA fire, but she was hit six times. Only the armoured flight deck saved her from sinking. The Fulmars shot eight enemy bombers down, but couldn't save their mother ship. Giant fires, fed by aviation fuel, roared through the hold. Many sailors were killed.

22:00: The *Illustrious* limped into the Grand Harbour, Malta, for emergency repairs, before being sent to the USA for a complete refit.

More Adventures for John

John Wellham went on to fight in the Battle of the Atlantic and against the Japanese in the Far East. He sur-

HMS *Illustrious*, on fire.

vived the war and wrote an exciting autobiography –
With Naval Wings. Put it on your reading list.

Back in the Atlantic
Meanwhile, back in the Atlantic the British were to face
a new horror. The *Bismarck* was ready for action.

BATTLE OF GIANTS – THE HUNT FOR THE *BISMARCK*

BATTLE BRIEFING

At the end of March 1941, the German surface raiders returned safely to their home ports (see chapter 1). Between them they had sunk or captured 48 ships, a total of almost 270,000 tons. Erich Raeder, Commander of the Kriegsmarine, hurried from port to port, congratulating the crews. He was so delighted with their success that he decided to play his ace card – the Bismarck.

The Bismarck was the most modern and powerful battleship in the world and could take on the best the British had to offer. She would be the ultimate surface raider. In early May she completed her proving trials and training exercises. It was time to turn her loose.

Bismarck – *Pride of the German Navy*

Builder: Blohm and Voss

Launched: 14 February 1939

Completed: 24 August 1940

Displacement: 41,673 tons; 49,136 fully loaded

Key armament: 8 15-inch guns (380 mm)

Max. Speed: 30 knots

Crew: 2,065

Bismarck – *The Break Out!*

5 May 1941: Adolf Hitler inspects the *Bismarck*

18 May: The *Bismarck* and the heavy cruiser *Prinz Eugen* sail in darkness from Gdynia in occupied Poland. Admiral Lutjens in command.

20 May: The *Bismarck* is spotted by a Swedish cruiser in

The *Bismarck* photographed just before the
breakout into the Atlantic.

the Skaggerak, the passage between Norway and Denmark. The news is leaked to British secret services.

21 May: The *Bismarck* is photographed by Spitfires at Bergen, Norway.

Key Mistake: The *Prinz Eugen* refuels, the *Bismarck* does not.

22 May: The *Bismarck* and *Prinz Eugen* slip away unseen, heading for the Denmark Straits between Iceland and Greenland. Beyond lie the open waters of the Atlantic. There are eleven helpless British convoys at sea.

Robert Tilburn, a Survivor's Story

Sleep!

Able Seaman Robert Tilburn closed his eyes and prayed for sleep. He was exhausted, his strength all but gone. Robert had clung to a tiny life raft about a metre square for what seemed like a lifetime. It was early summer but in these bitter Icelandic waters the cold had sunk into his bones.

He'd shivered at first, his body trying to protect itself. But the shivers had stopped a long time ago. The pain had gone too and he knew that was a bad sign.

Sleep!

He'd read that when you became really cold it was easy to fall asleep. It was meant to be a blessing. An easy way to die! And now that's all he wanted.

It was too much to take in. His mind was numb with shock.

A few minutes. That's all it had taken to sink the mighty *Hood*. Just minutes from the first shells screaming over. And then the terrible explosion. Two other sailors clung to rafts nearby – survivors like himself. But that was only three – three out of 1,419 men. Surely there had to be others?

The **Hood**'s Final Journey
22 May: Battleships the *Hood* and the *Prince of Wales* and six destroyers leave naval base at Scapa Flow in the Orkneys to trap the *Bismarck*. Vice Admiral Holland in command aboard the *Hood*.

The 'Mighty' Hood
Builder:	John Brown
Launched:	22 August 1918
Completed:	15 May 1920
Displacement:	42,462 tons; 48,360 fully loaded
Key Armament:	8 15-inch guns (380 mm)
Max. Speed:	29½ knots
Crew:	1,419

Problem: The *Prince of Wales* is brand-new and sails with workers still fixing her guns.

Last picture of HMS *Hood* taken
from HMS *Prince of Wales*.

23 May: Cruisers the *Norfolk* and the *Suffolk* are on patrol in the Denmark Straits.

19:22: The *Bismarck* and the *Prinz Eugen* spotted by the *Suffolk* as dusk falls. The two British ships use radar to shadow the German ships at a safe distance. Holland's force is 300 miles away and changes course to intercept. Intense radio traffic warns Germans that the British are closing in.

24 May, midnight: Admiral Holland hoists his battle ensign.

04:00: British ships are only 20 miles from raiders. The *Bismarck* picks up the sound of their engines on sonar. Lutjens puts the *Prinz Eugen* in the lead.

Key Mistake: 05:35: Holland closes in on the Germans at a fine angle – 280 degrees. Only the forward guns of his battleships can open fire.

Key Mistake: 05:49: Holland orders his force to open fire on the lead ship. He has mistaken the *Prinz Eugen* for the *Bismarck*.

05:52: The *Hood* opens fire – and misses.

Action Stations

Robert, like the rest of the *Hood*'s crew, had been eager for battle. This wasn't bravery, it was frustration. They had been at action stations since 22:00 the night before, dressed in anti-flash gear to protect them from burns – ghostly white gloves and hoods. Nerves were strained to the limit. The sooner it was over the better.

Robert was on the upper deck when the enemy came in range. He was part of the anti-aircraft gun crew and knew he would be little more than a witness to the coming fight. This was a ship-to-ship showdown, a battle of giants. Hood's huge 15-inch (380 mm) guns opened fire at 25,000 yards (20 km) and two minutes later the enemy replied – with amazing accuracy.

The second salvo from the *Prinz Eugen* straddled the *Hood* and a shell burst near Robert. He and two others rushed to tackle the fire but hadn't a hope. The heat triggered off the four-inch anti-aircraft ammunition stored in hopelessly thin steel lockers on the deck. As he threw himself flat to dodge the deadly fireworks the worst

47

minutes of his life began. While the deck fire flared, a far greater disaster was happening in the bowls of the *Hood*. The memory haunted him for years:

There was this dreadful explosion. It was most peculiar, the dead silence that followed it – I don't know if I was deaf. One of the other men by me was dead and another had his sides cut open and all his innards were tumbling out.

Shocked, Robert staggered to the ship's side to be sick. Instinct told him his ship was in trouble but he couldn't have guessed how badly. The mighty *Hood* was already dead. At 06:00, with the range down to ten miles (15 km), the *Bismarck* had fired a broadside. At least one shell, maybe more, plunged through the *Hood*'s main deck and exploded below the waterline. Almost immediately the magazines (the ammunition stores) ignited. Four-inch shells, 15-inch shells and torpedoes blew up in a catastrophic eruption that split the *Hood* in two. Most of the crew, heads down to their jobs in the engine room, the gun turrets, the bridge, had no warning that death had come to fetch them.

Out on deck, Robert had barely seconds to act. He threw off his tin hat, hood and gloves and made ready to swim for it. As the battleship broke up, the sea seemed to rise up to meet him. He plunged in, but the chill waters didn't bring safety. A broken yard arm smashed down and a flailing aerial wire tangled round his legs, pulling him down.

Fighting back panic, he recalled:

I cut my sea boots off with a knife and shot up like a cork out of a bottle. I must have been ten feet down by then. The ship was about 10 yards away from me, with her bows straight up in the air – and she just sank.

Rescue

In the suddenly empty ocean, Robert and the other two survivors, Signalman Albert Briggs and Midshipman Dundas, paddled towards one other. They each had the same grim thought in mind: 'If I'm going to die, please God, don't let me die alone.'

Shortly after the *Hood* went down their hopes were raised. A Sunderland flying boat passed overhead and they waved furiously, but the aircrew failed to spot them and flew on. It was another three endless hours before the destroyer *Electra* steamed in at high speed.

The *Electra* was one of the *Hood*'s own escorts, left behind in the dash to intercept the Germans. Her crew were stunned as they circled the battle zone – broken-hearted like children who had lost a mother. All they found of the great ship and her men was an oil slick, a few bits of wood – and three exhausted survivors. Nothing else human, not even bodies.

The **Bismarck** *Triumphant*

24 May, 06:00: The *Bismarck* and the *Prinz Eugen* concentrate their fire on the *Prince of Wales*.

The *Bismarck* down in the water and leaking oil after a
hit from a shell from the *Prince of Wales*.

06:13: The *Prince of Wales* breaks off the fight and
retreats under cover of smoke – hit seven times.
She has thirteen dead and many guns out of
action. Unknown to the British, the *Bismarck*'s
fuel lines are damaged, reducing her speed to 28
knots.

Key Mistake: Lutjens does not chase and finish the
Prince of Wales. He follows his orders to the letter and turns away to go after the convoys.

Closing the Net

24 May, morning: News of the *Hood* shocks Britain and
the Navy vows to take revenge. Ships across the Atlantic
are ordered to join the hunt. The *Prince of Wales*, the
Norfolk and the *Suffolk* turn and shadow the *Bismarck*.

Battleship *King George V*, battle-cruiser *Repulse* and aircraft carrier *Victorious* close in from the southeast. Battleship *Rodney* and six destroyers move in from the northeast. Force H – aircraft carrier *Ark Royal*, battle-cruiser *Renown* and cruiser *Sheffield* – join in the chase from Gibraltar.

18:00: The *Bismarck* and the *Prinz Eugen* split up. Lutjens is now so worried by the *Bismarck*'s shortage of fuel he decides to turn south to France for repairs. The *Prinz Eugen* breaks out into the Atlantic alone.

23:50: Eight Swordfish torpedo bombers from the aircraft carrier *Victorious* locate and attack the *Bismarck*. Only one torpedo hits and does little damage.

25 May, 01:30: The *Bismarck* and the *Prince of Wales* exchange fire.

03:06: Contact lost with the *Bismarck*. The British fear she has escaped.

Key Mistake: 08:54: Lutjens does not realize he has evaded the British and transmits a long report. Allied radio direction finders fix his position. The hunt is on again.

26 May, 10:30: A Coastal Command Catalina seaplane spots the *Bismarck* and signals her bearings to the fleet. But 31 hours have been lost – the *Bismarck* is way ahead of her pursuers.

14:50: Carrier *Ark Royal* launches a Swordfish attack,

now the only hope of slowing down the *Bismarck*.

15:40: Eleven planes dive on the target and launch their torpedoes. Luckily, all miss – they have attacked HMS *Sheffield*, the wrong ship!

19:10: The *Ark Royal* launches a second strike in rough seas and thick cloud.

20:47: The Swordfish begin a 40-minute attack on the *Bismarck*. Two torpedoes hit and wreck her steering gear. She slows to eight knots, only able to sail in huge slow circles. Amazingly, no British planes are shot down.

22:30, 26 May–07:00, 27 May: British destroyers play cat

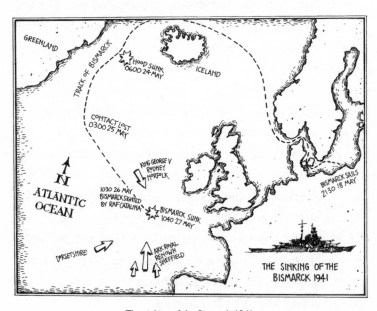

The sinking of the *Bismarck*, 1941.

52

Swordfish attacking the *Bismarck*.

and mouse through the night with the crippled *Bismarck*. Under heavy fire they launch sixteen torpedoes. All miss.

07:53: The *Norfolk* sights the *Bismarck*. The British fleet closes in for the kill.

08:47: The *Rodney* opens fire on the *Bismarck*, soon joined by the *Norfolk* and the *King George V*.

09:02: The *Bismarck*'s forward turrets put out of action.

09:31: All of the *Bismarck*'s guns out of action.

10:15: The *Bismarck* reduced to a burning hulk.

Hans Zimmerman, a Survivor's Story

Hans Zimmerman, a 20-year-old stoker, was stunned by the events of the past few days. On 24 May, the young crew of the *Bismarck* had cheered with delight when they sank the *Hood*. Now, only four days later, they were waiting for the Royal Navy to finish them off. Victory had turned into bitter defeat.

Hope ran out slowly. At first it looked as if they would make it to France for repairs – until the torpedo strike from the *Ark Royal* had jammed the rudders. Yet even then they were told that the *Bismarck* would be saved. Tankers and destroyers were on the way to tow them home, while U-boats and the Luftwaffe would keep the British battleships at bay. But in the end there was no rescue. Poor weather kept the Luftwaffe on the ground and the destroyers in port.

Hans recalled that the final enemy attack began at about 08:45. 'The battle, which lasted for 45 minutes, consisted of direct artillery fire. Since it was impossible for us to manoeuvre, the ship went round in circles. Then the order was given: "Blast open the sea-valves".'

The *Bismarck* had been 'smashed to pieces', but the hulk was to be sunk rather than left afloat as a trophy for the British.

When he was told to 'leave the ship by the shortest route', Hans began a nightmare journey through the ship. The superstructure had collapsed and a number of men were ripped apart by shells as they waited to escape. He and a few others crawled through a gap in the armour plating on to the upper deck.

'After a while,' Hans remembered, 'the *Bismarck* keeled over to port. We had civilians on board, about 25 of them. I watched one of them leap from the rail and break his neck. I was too much of a coward to jump.' Hans was lucky not to try. He had barely time to take off his combat gear and boots before the battleship sank. As she slipped beneath the waves he simply stepped off her into the sea, as easily as a bather into a swimming pool.

Certainly, Hans was luckier than Robert Tilburn. He was only in the water for 75 minutes before he was picked up by HMS *Dorsetshire*. The young German had feared capture by the British, but he was surprised by the care he was shown. 'On the *Dorsetshire* we were treated as equals . . . it was a case of 'you today, us tomorrow.'

Final Tragedy

27 May, 10:40: The *Bismarck* sunk. Cruiser *Dorsetshire* and destroyer *Maori* begin to haul survivors aboard. They have picked up 119 when a U-boat warning forces them to abandon the others. The *Dorsetshire* is a sitting target, her captain dare not wait. Hundred of Germans are left to die in the chill Atlantic.

19:00: *U-74* picks up three more survivors.

28 May, 10:35: Weather ship *Sachsenwald* finds two more

exhausted sailors in a life raft. They are the last. Over 2,000 of the *Bismarck*'s crew are dead.

FIGHTING FACTS

The Brilliant Bismarck

Named:	In honour of Count Otto von Bismarck, the nineteenth-century leader who had forged the German nation
Launched:	St Valentine's Day, 1939
Length:	820 ft (250 m), width 120 ft (37 m)
Armour:	Hardened Wotan steel 13 inches (33 cm) thick
Main gun turrets:	Four, each weighing 1,000 tons. Forward turrets were called Anton and Bruno, rear turrets Caesar and Dora
Average age of crew:	21
Codename for doomed Atlantic mission:	*Rheinubung* or 'Rhine Exercise'

The Tragedy of the Hood

The loss of the *Hood* was one of the greatest disasters suffered by the Royal Navy during World War II. After only eight minutes of firing, the great warship reared up with a broken back, her stern ribs blasted open by an enormous explosion. What on earth had happened?

Built Before Jutland

In 1941, the *Hood* was an old lady. She was laid down (begun) in 1916, during World War I. But crucially, she was designed before the Navy learned the lessons of the Battle of Jutland. At Jutland the two greatest fleets in the world fought one another and three British battle-cruisers were sunk by German fire. Long-range shells had plunged vertically through their thin deck armour, exploding inside their hulls.

After this all big warships were given thicker armour, but it was too late for the *Hood*. Her side armour was strengthened, but not her deck armour. When she took on the *Bismarck* that May morning, she was 'like a boxer with a glass jaw'. Once the German guns found her range she was finished. The *Prinz Eugen*'s gunnery officer, Commander Jasper, watched the *Hood* go down:

> *There was an explosion of incredible violence . . . Huge holes opened up in the grey hull and enormous flames leapt up from the depths of the ship . . . An ash-coloured pall of smoke formed two billowing columns. Below them rose a kind of incandescent dome.*

'Poor devils, poor devils!' he said out loud.

Survivors

Only three men survived the sinking of the *Hood*. One was Robert Tilburn, the others were Signalman Albert Briggs and Midshipman Dundas. Albert was on the bridge. He saw a vast sheet of flame and heard the officer of the watch report that the compass had gone. Then the ship fell sideways like a broken toy. He recalled:

> *I got out of the starboard door. By that time the water was level with the compass platform. I did not remember anything more until I found myself on the surface. The bows of the* Hood *were vertical in the water about 50 yards (45 m) away and I was looking at the bottom of the ship.*

The Amazing Luck of the Ark Royal

In 1941 the crew of the tiny *U-556* cheekily 'adopted' the *Bismarck* and promised to protect her from all dangers. This was a sailors' joke, made all the funnier by the mismatch in the size of the two vessels. How could a tiny submarine ever help such a giant battleship? Yet, weirdly, the pledge almost came true.

On 26 May *U-556* was returning to France after a successful attack on convoy HX 126. Suddenly she sighted two big British warships coming straight towards her – the *Ark Royal* and the *Renown*. The hunt for the *Bismarck* was so urgent that they had left their destroyer escorts behind in Gibraltar. They could not even spare the time to zigzag, the standard manoeuvre to avoid U-boats. They were sitting ducks!

However, when Captain Wohlfarth on *U-556* looked through his periscope he almost cried with frustration. He had fired all his torpedoes at the convoy. There was nothing he could do to stop the British. It was a tragedy for Germany but a marvellous piece of luck for Britain.

BULLDOG'S ENIGMA

BATTLE BRIEFING

The U-Boat Menace

If the German surface raiders were a shock to the British, it was their smaller, undersea, cousins who were deadlier. Winston Churchill wrote: 'The only thing that ever really frightened me during the war was the U-boat peril.'

U-boats were not true submarines in the modern sense – they were more like long-range torpedo boats, with the power to dive. To spot and catch their prey in an empty ocean U-boats had to cruise on the surface. At best they could spend little more than a day at a time underwater. The most common U-boat was the type VII 'Sea Wolf'. These had a range of 9785 miles (15,750 km) and a top speed of 17.5 knots on the surface and 7.5 submerged. They were armed with an 88-mm deck gun and fourteen torpedoes.

The British relied on technology. A growing number of con-

voy escorts were equipped with ASDIC (Allied Submarine Detection Investigation Committee). Invented in 1917, ASDIC was a sonar system that used sound waves to locate submerged U-boats. It transmitted a sound pulse which was reflected when it hit a solid object. The operator could detect this through headphones. Once the enemy's direction and depth were known, attacks could be made with depth-charges, dustbin sized canisters set to explode at different pressures as they sank. By 1941 radar was fitted to escort vessels so they could spot U-boats on the surface.

In the first four months of 1941 219 British ships had been sunk for the loss of only five German submarines. The British desperately needed a breakthrough.

The War of the Air Waves

Since the Battle of the Atlantic was fought across huge distances, commanders controlled their vessels by radio. To ensure secrecy both sides sent messages in codes. The Kriegsmarine believed that the U-boat codes were unbreakable, thanks to its Enigma cipher machines. These looked like a cross between an electric typewriter and a cash register. And they were fiendishly complicated.

Sets of whirling rotors gave each machine an almost uncountable number of settings for scrambling communications – almost six thousand million million million, according to one British expert. The German armed services used over 100,000 Enigmas to encode and decode messages during the war and every U-boat carried one.

In 1939 Britain set out to crack the secrets of the Engima. The centre for this crucial work was the Government Code and Cipher School at Bletchley Park, a country house 50 miles (80 km) northwest of London. As operations grew, the grounds became packed with hastily built huts. Hut 8 was the base of the team trying to read the German naval codes.

Each day a world-wide network of radio interception stations listened to even the faintest German signals. Painstakingly, every meaningless jumble of letters was noted down. These garbled messages were then sent to the code-breakers in Hut 8 who tried to find clues and patterns. They had some success but it often took three weeks to decipher a signal. What they needed was a change of fortune.

The stakes were high. If more convoys were to reach Britain safely, the Royal Navy had to know what the U-boats were doing. Or the war was lost!

The Hunter

U-Boat commander Lieutenant Julius Lemp had the instincts of a hunter. His reputation for skill, cunning and more than his fair share of good luck was made on the first day of the war. On Sunday, 3 September 1939, his submarine, *U-30*, was on patrol 250 miles (400 km) west of Ireland. A little after 13:00 the wireless operator handed him a signal: HOSTILITIES WITH BRITAIN TO BE OPENED IMMEDIATELY.

Germany was at war. Only hours later, he spotted his first kill.

At 21:00 Julius closed in on a large, blacked-out ship. The vessel was heading west from Britain, zigzagging at high speed to avoid detection.

'I know what you are, my friend,' he murmured.

Guessing that it was an armed merchant cruiser, Julius fired two torpedoes. Both struck home.

But Julius was wrong. He soon discovered his victim was the unarmed liner *Athenia*, carrying 1,100 passengers to Montreal. One hundred and twelve passengers died, including 28 Americans. It was a bloody start to the Battle of the Atlantic.

Julius was only 26 when he took command of *U-30*, but in the months that followed he became a U-boat ace. By August 1940 he had seventeen British ships to his score and a grateful Germany awarded him the Knight's Cross. Three months later he was rewarded again, this time with a new submarine, *U-110*. This was a large type IXB boat, 252.5 feet (78 m) long, with a range of 12,400 miles (20,000 km). It had a top speed of 18.2 knots on the surface and 7.3 submerged. Best of all, it carried 22 torpedoes, eight more than *U-30*.

With this magnificent weapon Lemp was confident of hitting the British hard. Sure enough, three weeks into his second patrol in *U-110* fortune smiled on him again. On Thursday, 8 May 1941, he saw smoke and the mast of a warship in the distance. Moving in for a closer look he found a fat target moving slowly across the lens of his periscope – Convoy OB 318.

The Prey

Atlantic Convoy OB 318 had left the safety of British
waters on 2 May 1941. Each convoy had a Navy designa-
tion – OB meant outward bound from Liverpool. The 38
ships in OB 318 sailed in nine short columns about 500
yards apart, like marching ranks of well-behaved school
children. The largest vessel was the steamer *Ixion* at
10,263 tons, the smallest the Dutch tug *Zwarte Zee*.
Since the convoy could only sail at the speed of the
slowest ship, usually 7–9 knots, discipline was vital. Ships
pulling ahead or lagging behind became easy targets for
U-boats. Wayward merchant captains were soon pulled
back into line by their Royal Navy chaperons.

As Lemp watched OB 318 with predatory eyes, others were on a mission to protect the convoy. Circling

A RAF pilot's view of a vulnerable
North Atlantic convoy.

like protecting sheepdogs were the 3rd Escort Group, a mixed bag of warships: three destroyers – *Bulldog*, *Amazon* and *Broadway*, the armed liner *Ranpura*, and three tiny flower-class corvettes: *Aubretia*, *Hollyhock* and *Nigella* (see Fighting Facts). The pretty names of the corvettes seemed at odds with their deadly purpose – they were U-boat killers.

The commander of the escort flotilla was Joe Baker-Cresswell, captain of the *Bulldog*. Joe was born in London

Captain Joe Baker-Cresswell,
May 1941.

on 2 February 1901 while most of his family was watching the funeral procession of Queen Victoria. He joined the Navy in 1919 and served in every type of ship from battle-wagons to submarines. He was appointed to 3rd Escort Group in January 1941 and soon turned it into one of the best units in the Atlantic. Typically, after careful testing, he chose unique camouflage colours for his ships – pale mauve in spring and summer and white in winter.

Joe's force had taken over care of OB 318 on Wednesday 7 May. They met the convoy in the mid-Atlantic, at a rendezvous point 150 miles (240 km) south of Iceland. And sailed straight into trouble. At 19:00 another prowling submarine, *U-94*, sneaked between the columns of ships and fired three torpedoes. One missed but two struck home. The big British steamer *Ixion* and the *Eastern Star* from Norway burst into flames and sank quickly. The *Bulldog* led the frantic search for *U-94*, launching salvos of depth charges, but as the time passed it was clear the enemy had escaped. Joe was left feeling angry and helpless, but he had done better than he knew. The submarine commander later reported: 'Subjected to very severe and accurate counterattacks which lasted four hours and caused considerable damage.'

Lemp Strikes
Early on the morning of Friday 9 May Joe had just begun

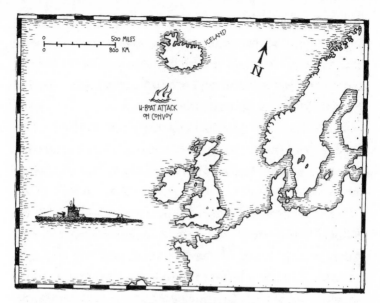

The attack on OB 318.

to relax. OB 318 was now well past Iceland, at longitude 34 degrees west – and there had never been any attacks that far into the Atlantic. But the nightmare was about to begin again. Julius Lemp was closing in.

Julius had shadowed the convoy through the night and as dawn broke, manoeuvred to attack. By noon he was ready. At periscope depth, *U-110* fired three torpedoes from the front, starboard side of OB 318. The range was 800 yards. The first victim was the *Esmond*. From the bridge of the *Bulldog* Joe watched in horror as a spout of water rose over the ship, the telltale mark of an explosion below the waterline. Almost at once the stern of the *Esmond* lifted into the air and her deck cargo of trucks and cases tumbled into the sea. It looked, a witness wrote, 'like a child pouring toys out of a box'. As she slowly sank, another torpedo struck the *Bengore Head* amidships and broke her back.

Third Escort Group burst into a flurry of activity. The *Bulldog* tore away from the convoy as Joe shouted orders. He had a hunch where the submarine might be. But it was the *Aubretia* that wreaked revenge first. At 12:03 the corvette spotted a periscope and gained an ASDIC echo, about half a mile away. Dashing in, she dropped a pattern of depth charges set to explode between 100 and 225 feet (30 m and 70 m) down.

Julius was shaken by the speed of the counterattack. He had reckoned on at least ten minutes to escape.

'Down Deep,' he yelled, the order for an emergency dive.

It was too late. A score of depth charges exploded around *U-110*, stopping her electric motors and damaging the hull. The stunned submariners looked about in horror as she began to take in water and sank even deeper. Her plates groaned and cracked with the pressure. With British warships circling overhead Lemp had two choices: stay down and die – or surface and abandon ship.

He chose life for his men and blew the tanks.

The first the crew of the *Aubretia* knew of her success was a ferment on the choppy Atlantic swells. Then, to

U-110.

their astonishment, a U-boat burst up, water streaming from the conning tower. Almost at once the hatch opened. There was a fountain of pressurized dust and the Germans began to clamber out.

On the bridge of his destroyer Joe saw red. He ordered the *Bulldog* up to 12 knots. Ramming speed! And headed for the submarine. His forward guns opened fire and the first shell was a direct hit. Yet almost at once he thought again. What were the Germans doing? My God! It looked as if they were abandoning ship. Might it just be possible he could capture a U-boat?

The Fortunes of War

The next few minutes were a whirl of confusion and mistakes on both sides. Joe brought the *Bulldog* to a halt only 100 metres from *U-110* but now the *Broadway* was closing fast. He grabbed a megaphone and yelled, 'Keep Clear!' At the last moment she swung away but not before she dropped two depth charges under the submarine, to stop it diving again. By now the U-boat was surrounded by Navy ships and a torrent of small arms and machine-gun fire tore into the escaping German crew. Several were killed before Joe's frantic order to 'cease fire' was obeyed.

On the bridge of *U-110* Julius watched in horror as the *Broadway* bore down.

'Out! Out! The destroyer is going to ram us,' he shouted.

In the hurry to escape a vital rule was broken. The young radio operator, Heinz Wilde, left behind the top-secret Enigma machine and code-books. He knew his orders. They must not be captured at any cost! The books were even printed with water soluble ink so they would be unreadable as soon as they hit the sea.

But orders are one thing and survival is another. The Enigma was bolted to the table. It would take a minute or more to unfasten it. Heinz believed he had only seconds before the submarine was rammed and sunk. He got out – FAST!

Julius Lemp followed the empty-handed radio operator over the side but he wasn't worried. He was certain *U-110* was doomed and a sunken ship could tell no secrets. If she survived the charge of the destroyer, she would be blown apart by the explosives he had just set. These charges were built into every U-boat – a self-destruct system to prevent capture.

What happened next is a mystery. Julius must have watched grimly as the *Broadway* changed course – almost too late. The two vessels collided and the submarine's after (rear) **hydroplane** sliced open the destroyer's forward, port, tank. Oil poured into the water, adding to the misery of his crew. Worse, he must have sensed the minutes ticking by.

Minutes used by the Navy to pick up German survivors.

And minutes during which a boarding party from the *Bulldog* began to row towards *U-110*.

Slowly Julius must have realized that THE EXPLOSIVE CHARGES WERE NOT GOING TO FIRE. Most likely the detonators had failed to go off. Not his fault. An error. An error too far! No one saw him die – and his body was never recovered. Some say he was so ashamed that he committed suicide by allowing himself to drown. Others argue that he tried to reboard his boat, determined to blow the charges, and was shot as he climbed aboard.

Joe Baker-Cresswell was almost as stunned as Julius Lemp when *U-110* survived the attack by the *Broadway*.

'Organize a boarding party instantly, put Balme in charge,' he ordered.

When 20-year-old Sub-lieutenant David Balme

reported to the bridge, Joe told him, 'Take the whaler (small rough weather boat). Your job is to secure all important papers, ciphers, charts – anything that you can find.'

Little did David know he was about to change the course of the war.

A Steel Coffin

With a party of seven men David rowed over to *U-110* – and his problems began almost at once. In the rough seas there was no easy way to fasten the tiny boat to the submarine. Eventually, chancing his luck, the bowman leapt aboard and secured a line. Yet, almost as soon as the others clambered out, a wave picked up the boat and jammed it between the conning tower and guard rails. Further waves quickly smashed it to pieces. For the time being they were stranded on the U-boat.

Worried but determined, David got on with the job. Leading the way, he entered the submarine, wondering if this would be his last action. His thoughts ran riot:

Was the U-boat about to blow up and become his steel coffin? Was the sea already rushing in through plates damaged by the depth-charge attacks? Were German stragglers, perhaps Nazi fanatics, waiting with loaded weapons?

Breathing deeply, he resisted the urge to throw in a hand grenade.

To David's relief, he found the emergency lights still

on. The control room was bathed in an eerie blue glow but thankfully seemed deserted. Everywhere there were signs of the crew's hasty escape – even a half-eaten plate of shrimps in the radio room. David called in the others and they began a systematic search of the boat. He wrote later:

> The telegraphist (Allen Long) went to the wireless office, noted all the settings and dismantled a lot of equipment. Two or three seamen helped me pass the charts up through the conning tower and these were soon followed by all the books. We lost all sense of time.

For Joe Baker-Cresswell, however, each minute seemed like an age. He sent the *Bulldog*'s motor boat to replace the wrecked whaler, then all he could do was watch and pray. David's boarding party formed a human chain to off-load their precious loot, but they were buffeted like gangly puppets in the rough weather. Again and again sailors slithered, skidded and bumped along the U-boat deck. Joe waited for the fateful slip – man overboard, vital information lost – but amazingly every armful made it into the boat. For four long hours *U-110* was stripped of anything useful and the material ferried to the *Bulldog*.

Not surprisingly, the sailors helped themselves to rare treats – cigarettes, cigars, tinned ham, corned beef, beer. David pocketed a set of Super Zeiss binoculars and found them the best he had ever used.

By midnight the work was done. *U-110* was battened down and taken under tow – but the prize was to slip away. At 10:50 the next morning she reared her bows and sank slowly by the stern. The tow line was cut with an axe and the submarine slipped away. Joe was gutted. Another day and they would have pulled her safely into Iceland. Still, he consoled himself, there were two large crates of equipment and papers in the hold of the *Bulldog*. Joe had a suspicion they'd grabbed something special but couldn't have realized how right he was.

Reward for Risks

When *U-110* sank, so did the evidence that she had been captured. Her crew knew little or nothing. They had been rescued by the *Aubretia* and the *Broadway*, hustled below decks and rushed out of sight. None escaped back to Germany. Ironically, had Joe been able to tow the submarine into an Allied base, she may have been spotted by an enemy plane or another U-boat. As it was the Germans had no reason to think that *U-110* had been captured.

Soon after the *Bulldog* put into Scapa Flow in Scotland, intelligence officers came aboard. At first they couldn't believe their eyes. They had arrived with only a briefcase to take away the important items and found themselves overwhelmed with riches. As they looked through the crates one gloated to David Balme, 'This is what we've been looking for.'

The Enigma machine still had the settings for 9 May on its rotors. Better still were the code books, with the daily settings for three months up to the end of June.

Every page was photographed in case of accidents and the treasure trove flown to Bletchley Park. For months

An Enigma code machine.

the code-breakers in Hut 8 had been struggling to read the German Navy code they had nicknamed 'Hydra'. The *Bulldog* 'catch' was like a beam of light in a dark cellar. By 1 June the Hut 8 team were deciphering Hydra signals almost as fast as the Germans.

The effect on the war came quickly. In June 1941 U-boats sank 61 ships. In July this fell to 23 and stayed low for most of the year. The Royal Navy Submarine Tracking Room at Liverpool was responsible for routing convoys. With information flooding in from Bletchley Park, they were able to guide them away from enemy locations. Joe Baker-Cresswell was never told the full importance of his capture of *U-110* until years after the war. But he was given a hint. In early June he received a signal from Sir Dudley Pound, the First Sea Lord: HEARTIEST CON-GRATULATIONS. THE PETALS OF YOUR FLOWERS ARE OF RARE BEAUTY.

FIGHTING FACTS

Flower Power

The *Aubretia*, the escort that forced *U-110* to the sur-face, was a 'flower'-class corvette. Although tiny, these fighting ships bore the brunt of the Battle of the Atlantic. Design: Based on a whale catcher. Originally built to guard coastal convoys

Top Speed: Only 16.5 knots

Armament:	One 4-inch gun (102 mm) and 40 depth charges (later increased to 72) fired from launchers or rolled from the stern
Crew Comments:	'Rolled like pigs in rough seas', 'Cold miserable and damp', 'In winter the open bridge was thick with ice – we spent hours chipping ice away.'
Insults:	The names of the flower-class corvettes led to their crews being the butt of other sailors' humour. Is that a periscope over there? Better send for *Bluebell*. No, no, it's a job for *Clover*.

U-boat Captains – the Ace of Aces

Julius Lemp, captain of *U-110*, was good – he sank 23 ships, 97,000 tons. Even so, he came way down the list of U-boat Aces. The top scorer was Otto Kretschmer:

Profile of an Ace

Born:	1912
Nickname:	The 'tonnage king'
Total Sank:	44 ships, more than 250,000 tons
Favourite method of attack:	On the surface, at night. One torpedo fired at point-blank range.
Favourite targets:	Why look for trouble? Most of his

	victims were ships travelling on their own, rather than in convoy
Notable Victims:	Armed cruisers *Petroculus*, *Laurentic* and *Forfar*, sunk in November and December 1940
Captured:	March 1941 when his boat, *U-99*, was sunk by the destroyer *Walker*

Air Power – the Key to Victory

In 1943 the odds turned against the U-boats due to aeroplanes and aircraft carriers.

Guardian angels

Long-range aircraft Liberators, Sunderlands and Catalinas patrolled convoy routes from bases in Northern Ireland, Newfoundland and Iceland.

Equipment: Radar, searchlights, machine-guns and depth charges. Very effective U-boat killers.

Escort Carriers

The first of these mini aircraft carriers was HMS *Audacity*, launched in 1941. Believe it or not, she was a converted banana boat! But it was another two years before there were enough escort carriers in service to make a difference. They flew a variety of planes including Hawker Hurricanes, Fairey Swordfish, and Gruman Avengers.

Secret Weapon

By April 1943 Allied planes had a new, secret weapon – the Mark 24 Mine. Just to complicate matters, this wasn't a mine at all. The name was a cover to hide its true purpose. The Mark 24 was a homing torpedo – it tracked the noise of a U-boat's propeller. In total 346 were dropped and about a third of them hit home – 67 U-boats were sunk and 33 damaged.

U-Boats Blitzed

The effect of air power was shown dramatically in 1944. Only 31 Allied ships were sunk in the North Atlantic but the Kriegsmarine paid dearly – over 200 U-boats were destroyed.

The Final Cost

The U-boat campaign in the North Atlantic sank almost 3,000 Allied ships, weighing more than 14 million tons. At least 30,000 merchant seamen died.

At first the U-boats had the upper hand but by 1944 the life expectancy of a German submariner was 50 days. Out of 820 U-boats, 718 were destroyed in action: some 32,000 crewmen died.

U-boat Graveyard

When the war ended Britain, America and the Soviet Union agreed that all captured U-boats would be sunk to stop them ever being used again. There are 116 lying in an eerie U-boat cemetery off Malin Head, Ireland. Scrap dealers have their eye on them. Each one contains about 750 tons of steel, brass and copper – worth around £400,000 at 1996 prices.

Could you have cracked the Enigma?

Are you an oddball? A computer nerd? Got a razor-sharp mind?

In the dark days of 1941 Bletchley Park needed you. To find people with quirky thinking, an unusual recruiting campaign was launched at the end of 1941. Readers of the *Daily Telegraph* were asked how long they took to finish the paper's crossword. Half an hour? Hopeless! How about less than 12 minutes?

Twenty-five puzzle freaks who took up the challenge were invited to take part in a timed competition. The fastest was Mr Vere Chance from Orpington who finished in 6 min 3.5 seconds. Sadly he had spelt a word wrong and was disqualified. Four others completed the puzzle within 12 minutes, the quickest being Mr Hawes from Dagenham in 7 min 57.5 seconds.

A few weeks later those involved received a letter marked 'Confidential'. They were called to interviews with MI8 – the military intelligence department in charge of Bletchley Park. If they passed they were asked to train as code-breakers. One was Stanley Sedgewick. He recalled: 'I think I was told, though not so bluntly, that chaps with twisted brains like mine might be suitable for a particular type of war work.' Stanley ended up in the Air Section breaking German weather codes. Boring?? No way. German weather reports were used to help Bomber Command plan raids over Europe.

THE BLOODY BEACHES OF DIEPPE

BATTLE BRIEFING

In June 1940, even as British troops were escaping from the beaches of Dunkirk, Winston Churchill promised: 'Britain will fight on. We shall go back.'

But 'going back' – the invasion of Nazi-dominated Europe – took four long years.

The Commandos Strike Back

At first, the best the Allies could do was a series of pinprick raids by commandos and paratroopers. The most spectacular was the attack on the French port of Saint Nazaire, in March 1942. The Navy wanted the large dry docks there destroyed, before they could be used as a base for the battleship Tirpitz. *She was the Bismarck's sister ship and every bit as deadly. (See chapter 6.) The old destroyer* Campbeltown, *packed with 4.5 tons explosives, fought her way into the har-*

bour. The Germans didn't know it, but she was a floating time bomb. When the Campbeltown blew up at 11:30 on 28 March, the docks were wrecked and 400 Nazi troops killed. But the raid was costly – of 611 commandos and sailors involved, 397 were killed or captured.

Invasion Rehearsal

Inspired by St Nazaire, Allied planners decided to seize and hold a French port for about twelve hours. There were several reasons for doing this. The Americans were beginning a massive build up of troops in Britain and wanted to launch the invasion of Europe by the end of 1942.

Meanwhile, the Russian leader Stalin was desperate. His troops were facing the full might of the German army – and losing. He wrote anxiously to Churchill: 'It seems to me that the military situation of the Soviet Union (Russia) . . . would be greatly improved if there was a second front against Hitler in the West.'

Churchill, however, was worried. He wanted to test the enemy defences to see what problems came up – before risking a full-scale assault.

Target Dieppe

The target for this 'test' was Dieppe. It was chosen because the Allies knew they had to capture a port to resupply their armies during the real invasion. But could one be taken? How well dug-in were the Germans? What were the likely casualties? The results were far worse than expected. Those who

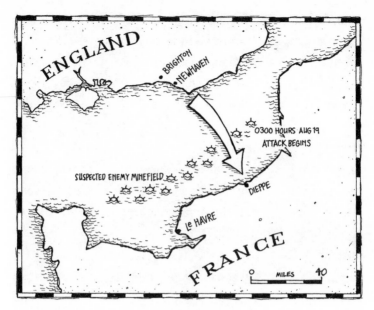

The Dieppe raid.

survived used words like 'slaughter', 'fiasco' and 'mayhem' to describe their experiences.

On 18 August 1942, 6,100 men, mostly Canadians, set off across the Channel. From the start the raid went wrong. The flotilla blundered into a German convoy and any chance of surprise was lost. Worse, Dieppe itself was very well-defended. The Germans had guns mounted on the headlands and had turned the hotels along the elegant promenade into blockhouses (strong points).

The first troops hit the beaches at 05:10 and ran into a storm of fire. Fifteen Churchill tanks fought their way over the high sea wall and on to the esplanade. But they soon found

Allied troops fight their way ashore.

they were trapped. Trooper Dick Clarke recalled: 'We went round in circles, using up our ammo, using up our gas, being shelled and rolling over people.'

At 10:50 the withdrawal began behind a smoke screen dropped by the RAF. The final cost was 1,027 dead and 2,340 left behind as prisoners.

Jack Brewin – Special Sea Service Veteran
One survivor of Dieppe was Jack Brewin. Jack had joined the Royal Marines in 1941 and trained for duties with the Special Sea Service. He was told that he was to be a gunner on a new and highly secret type of vessel – a landing craft.

These were 'the brainchild of Winston Churchill himself ... (and designed) to head the actual assaults planned for Europe'.

Like all the Marines he wanted to serve on a large warship. 'The bigger the ship,' he recalled, 'the more one had to be proud of.' Imagine his disappointment then when he first saw LCF (L) 5 (Landing Craft Flak – an anti-aircraft ship). The LCF was squat and ugly, and rolled violently in heavy seas. The crew accommodation was tiny: '50 odd of us crammed into a space 50' x 12'. We were never able to all mess (eat) or sleep at the same time. The officers were crammed into a space originally designed for the toilets. The engineers actually lived and slept with their engines.'

The only good thing about her was her weapons. LCF (L) 5 bristled with Pom-Pom (anti-aircraft) guns and **Oerlikon** cannon.

Jack's memories of Dieppe are striking. This is his story, told in his own words:

Landing Craft at Dieppe

Newhaven

LCF 5 provided support for the 4th Landing Craft Flotilla. We knew that something big was about to take place. The jetty soon became crowded with troops, for the most part Canadians but also No. 3 Commando. A Surgeon Commander came aboard carrying an ominous black bag (his surgical instruments).

On the afternoon of 18 August, things really began to

take shape. I think our own force left Newhaven at 01:00 hours. It was a very dark night, the sea was swelly and no lights were visible. We were under strict orders not to open fire, even at suspicious targets. Movement was very hazardous in the dark. There were several near misses between craft and we barely missed an LCT (Landing Craft Tank – a tank carrier) which was beam on (sideways) to our approach.

We were at action stations all the time and I was gun layer on No. 2 pom-pom (anti-aircraft gun). When I cast my mind back, I remember feeling very lonely. I was not afraid of what lay ahead, I don't think any of us were, but we had time to think about what might be in wait for us. The average age of the crew was 19 to 20 and none of us had seen active service before. I was just 19½.

At about 03:00 hours the sky filled with tracer shot and it was obvious that we were under attack. We altered course to starboard and left the action behind. Now we had the bad luck to run into a small German convoy. This contributed to the terrible outcome of the operation.

As dawn broke we had our first glimpse of the hostile shore. Strangely it seemed quite normal. I saw some white cliffs and a town and, apart from some distant thuds, nothing seemed unusual. However, as the morning light grew I began to see the size of the operation. The foreshore was littered with dozens of craft and the sea was covered in ships (252 altogether).

Maybe it wasn't like I now imagine, but it seemed that with the coming of full light the scene changed. The air was suddenly full of aircraft and we fired madly at them. We were about half a mile (1 km) from the shore and were so busy with our guns that whatever was happening on the beach escaped us.

We fought off the planes for about two hours. There appeared to be hundreds of aircraft everywhere and identification was difficult. We just fired at everything that came near. When a plane was shot down we all

GERMAN MESSERSCHMITT 109

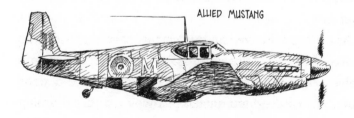

ALLIED MUSTANG

Could you tell the difference in the heat of battle?

cheered and claimed a kill. That day the RAF were oper-
ating Mustang fighters for the first time, and they looked
so like the German Messerschmitt 109 that we almost
certainly shot one down.

White Beach

It was about 08:30 when we steamed closer to the
shore to cover the withdrawal of the landing from
'White Beach'. What we had experienced so far under
air attack was nothing to the holocaust we saw now.
Landing craft, mostly LCPs (Landing Craft Personnel)
were streaming back from the beach, packed with badly
wounded men. Our own craft lay all but on the beach,
broadside on and it seemed that every gun, light and
heavy, was directed on us from the shore. I was rooted
to the gun platform, possibly because I imagined the
shield would give me some protection. Then the gun
jammed.

Tracer flew in all directions and a great piece of metal
from the ship's side landed at my feet. I heard terrible
screams all around me as the wounded were being lifted
aboard. The sights were ghastly – a Canadian minus an
arm climbed aboard unaided, calmly smoking a cigarette.
I wouldn't have believed such courage. There were terri-
bly mutilated bodies all around. The sea was full of debris
and floating dead, the air full of stinking smoke. I remember looking towards the bridge, seeking some renewal
of strength from our officers – and seeing nothing but
white faces as frightened as my own.

The officers' mess deck (mess deck – eating area) was used as a sick bay and the orderlies (paramedics) were almost throwing the wounded down to the surgeon. He was faced with an impossible task of mercy that day. At the same time the dead were being laid out on the deck. One of the Canadians was covered in a Union Jack found inside his jacket – surely not the purpose for which it had been carried.

I have no idea how long this terrible episode lasted, it must have been several hours. The ship's guns were now all out of action and our only purpose was as some misplaced haven for those returning from the beaches. A Canadian actually tumbled aboard, cursing and screaming, before he turned around and dived back into the sea. It all added to the general impression of noise, smoke and utter disaster. The British destroyer *Berkeley* was very close to us when she was bombed and sunk.

Retreat

Orders were eventually given for our withdrawal. I have no idea of the actual time, but we were among the last to leave. A wave of Boston bombers swept in very low as we left. The skies were now clear of enemy planes but the fire from the shore was still active until we were out of range. A heavy cloud of smoke enveloped the town, the beach was filled with crippled tanks and landing craft. (The smoke bombs had been dropped by the RAF to cover the retreat.)

The returning force must have looked a sorry sight.

We were all bearing the scars of battle and even now I noticed craft sinking or being abandoned. A gun boat slid alongside us and transferred a German pilot picked out of the sea. He was naked apart from a blanket and some of the Canadian survivors attempted to kill him before being restrained. He was locked up in a paint store, little larger than a cupboard, for his own safety.

The journey back was one of complete misery. The mess deck was crowded with survivors and the wounded lay everywhere – a stench of mutilated humanity prevailed. I was in a state of shock. I lay on the deck and tried to gather myself together. We arrived off Newhaven late at night only to find that the defence nets had been drawn and the harbour blocked. We had to remain outside all night despite our plight, with all the wounded aboard. A very cold welcome back indeed. Next morning the wounded were loaded into ambulances which lined the Quayside. Our poor dead were hoisted ashore on large, flat boards by dockside cranes. This seemed so unfeeling somehow.

I had no idea what our role had been. I knew even less of what had been achieved – if anything. Later a war correspondent came aboard and asked me, 'What did you think of Dieppe?'

'So that's where we've been,' I replied.

How ridiculous that must have sounded to him – but the name meant nothing to me.

British newspapers took an optimistic stance to the Dieppe raid.

FIGHTING FACTS

Mountbatten Takes the Blame

Lord Louis Mountbatten, cousin of King George VI, was appointed Chief of Combined Operations in March 1942. His job was to make sure Allied armies, navies and airforces worked closely together, instead of squabbling. He always accepted the blame for Dieppe – and never regretted the attack. He wrote:

> The Duke of Wellington said that the Battle of
> Waterloo was won on the playing fields of Eton and
> I say that the Battle of Normandy (the invasion of
> Europe) was won on the beaches of Dieppe.

Mountbatten wasn't being callous. He believed the mistakes made at Dieppe taught the Allies vital lessons that saved many thousands of lives on D-Day (6 June 1944), the first day of the invasion. Lessons like these:

Lessons Learned at Dieppe

Mistake: Dieppe was far more strongly defended than expected.

Lesson Learned: Don't attack an enemy harbour head on from the sea. Too many men will die and the harbour itself will be too damaged to be much use afterwards. Invade Europe on isolated beaches, where defences are weaker.

On D-Day: The Allies took two prefabricated harbours

with them. Codenamed 'Mulberries', they were made from huge caissons – hollow concrete blocks each weighing hundreds of tons. They were anchored off the Normandy beaches and worked well until wrecked by a storm on 18 June.

Mistake: The German airforce fought well and used a new fighter, the Focke Wulf 190A, for the first time. The RAF was shocked. Their Spitfires were outclassed and they did not have command of the air during the raid.

Lesson Learned: Allied airforces must destroy the Luftwaffe and have 'air superiority' over the invasion sites.

On D-Day: The German airforce was broken in huge battles by long-range American fighters during January–April 1944. On 6 June the Luftwaffe only flew 319 sorties (missions or flights) during the whole day, the Allies flew 14,674.

Mistake: Bombers were not used against Dieppe so as to avoid causing heavy casualties amongst French civilians.

Lesson Learned: Enemy defences must be pounded from the air by heavy bombers, before the troops hit the beaches. Some civilian deaths must be accepted.

On D-Day: 1,056 Lancasters, Halifaxs and Mosquitoes dropped 5,000 tons of bombs on German gun batteries near the Allied landing zones.

Mistake: The Dieppe raid was only backed by eight destroyers. They could not offer enough supporting fire for the troops struggling to fight their way off the beaches.

Lesson Learned: The invasion must be supported by massive fire power from the sea, including battleships.

On D-Day: 1,213 warships, most of them British and Canadian, protected thousands of landing craft. It was the greatest armada in history.

Special Forces

Commandos

Ten 'Commando' units, each 500 strong, were formed in 1940. Their mission was to strike back at Hitler's 'fortress Europe'. They took their name from the Boer guerrilla fighters of the South African War (1899–1902) and were amongst the toughest troops in the British forces.

Training took place at Achnacarry Castle, near Fort William in Scotland. Recruits arrived after a ten-mile route march – and were greeted with a mock graveyard. This was said to hold the bodies of those who died during the tough course. Commandos learned how to use explosives, how to attack from the sea in a variety of boats – everything from canoes to landing craft – and how to kill silently, at close quarters, with their famous dagger.

The tools of the commandos' trade.

Eyewitness Ray Bromley trained at Achnacarry in 1941. He recalled:

Everything had to be done at the double – no walking was permitted. Reveille was at 06:00, when we had to dress in trousers, boots gaiters and belt, but no shirt whatever the weather. Then came PT (physical training) which consisted of tossing telegraph poles at each other in teams. Washing facilities were simply metal bowls set out on wooden tables along a stream, the ice had to be broken first.

Paratroops

Churchill had been impressed by the German glider and paratroops in 1940. In Holland, they had captured the crucial fort of Eban Emal by landing on the roof. He gave orders to train 'a corps of at least 5,000 parachute troops' and first units were ready by late 1941.

Great Special Forces Raids

Date	Place	Mission
4 March 1941	Lofoten Islands, Norway	Commandos blew up factories producing cod and herring oil. (Blowing up fish oil? Sounds fishy, but the oil was used for vitamin pills for German troops and to make glycerine for explosives.)
27 December 1941	Vaagso, Norway	Commandos damaged the port and forced Hitler to station more troops in Norway.
27 February 1942	Bruneval, France	Paratroops snatched parts of a top-secret German Wurzburg radar set. As a bonus they captured one of the radar operators.
26 March 1942	St Nazaire, France	Commandos aboard the *Campbeltown* destroyed gun emplacements and the pumps that operated the dry docks.
19 August 1942	Dieppe, France	Commandos destroyed the 'Hess' gun battery to the west of the town. This was the only real success of the raid.
7 December 1942	Bordeaux, France	Raiders in canoes attached limpet mines to nine German merchant ships. Known as the Cockleshell heroes, only two escaped out of a force of ten.

THE X-CRAFT AND THE BEAST

BATTLE BRIEFING

The Beast

The Tirpitz, *sister ship of the* Bismarck, *was an awesome vessel. She weighed 52,600 tons fully laden and was armed with eight 15-inch (380 mm) guns, in four twin turrets. Like the* Bismarck, *she was almost the length of three football fields, 120 feet (37 m) wide at the beam and ten stories high from keel to bridge. Winston Churchill gave her a sinister nickname – 'the beast'.*

In September 1943 the *Tirpitz* skulked in her icy lair in northern Norway. And what a lair it was – a bleak natural fortress made stronger by German military engineers. Allied air photographs and Norwegian spies presented daunting reports. The *Tirpitz* rested in an impregnable berth at the top of Kaafjord, a finger of the much longer Altenfjord, 30 miles (50 km) from the open sea. Nearby lay the pocket battleships *Scharnhorst* and *Lutzow* and an escort of ten destroyers. Together they made a mighty fleet.

The Germans were playing a brilliant game. The *Tirpitz* did not even have to fight to be a threat. She simply had to sit there – a day's sailing from the Allied convoy route to Russia. Even a rumour that she was about to sail was enough to dismay the Royal Navy. The last thing the British wanted was another disaster like the breakout of the *Bismarck*. A strong force with an aircraft carrier, and at least two battleships, had to be kept within striking distance of Norway. Just in case.

In August 1943, Churchill wrote a worried letter to the Russian leader, Joseph Stalin:

The Germans have concentrated in the Arctic a powerful battle fleet. The danger to Russian convoys which I described to you last year has returned in even more menacing form. If one or two of our battleships were to be lost, or even seriously damaged, while the Tirpitz remained in action, the whole command of the Atlantic would be jeopardized.

Closer to home, Churchill had already sent a blunt message to his own admirals: 'Sink or damage that damn ship.'

Stalking the Beast

But it was easier said than done. Kaafjord was north of

the Arctic Circle, beyond the range of British heavy bombers. Raids by carrier-based planes would have been little better than suicide missions. Dive-bombers like the Swordfish faced the risk of crashing into the steep fjord sides – if they managed to avoid the countless flak batteries and vigilant Luftwaffe fighters.

Attacks from the sea would have fared little better. The entrance to Altenfjord, through Stjern Sound, was sealed with minefields, while Kaafjord was barricaded with an anti-submarine net. This was made of steel wire and woven into a tight mesh that could bring a 1,500-ton sub to a grinding halt. Inside, close to the hull of the *Tirpitz* were the anti-torpedo nets, able to stop a torpedo travelling at 50 miles an hour. Radar, searchlights, smoke-screens, patrol boats and shore batteries added to the mind-blowing problems.

And then there was the *Tirpitz* herself. Her steel hull was designed to withstand the most powerful shells and torpedoes, while at the waterline an extra steel belt 6 feet (2 m) wide and 15 inches (35 cm) thick ran most of her length. What on earth could be done to destroy this invincible ship?

A New Weapon

For the past 18 months the Navy had been working on an answer, a deadly flotilla of midget submarines – the top-secret X-craft. And by the autumn of 1943 they were ready for action.

A reconnaissance shot of *Tirpitz* safely tucked behind her nets at Kaafford.

Secret!
Deadly!
Ready!

This was the language Churchill relished. 'Use them as soon as possible,' he ordered.

The new subs were just under 50 feet (15 m) long and weighed 35 tons, with a top speed of about 6½ knots on the surface and five knots submerged. Their cramped hulls barely had room for a crew of four but they could still dive to a depth of 300 feet (90 m). And for their size, they carried a colossal punch. Instead of torpedoes the X-craft were armed with two detachable mines, each holding 2 tons of amatex explosive.

They would need it. They were going after an enemy a thousand times their size.

The X-Project

The prototype, *X-3*, had been launched secretly at 23:00 on 19 March 1942. For the next few weeks she went through exhaustive trials in Portland Harbour. Her base was a specially built floating shed with two hulls. *X-3* berthed between them, secure from prying eyes. While she was under test, the Navy began to select crewmen.

The call went out for men 'for special and hazardous duty' and there was no shortage of volunteers. One of the first, John Lorimer, later on the *X-6*, recalled:

If you are going to do anything dangerous, the best way to do it is to train, train, train, so that in the excitement of the action you do the thing automatically. I cannot overemphasize the drilling they put us through, the importance of it, the fact that none of us minded. Rank? . . . We lived like pirates, called one another by our

Christian names, but the discipline was complete. When
an order was given, it was immediately carried out.

Over the next year, six more improved X-craft were
built and shipped to Loch Cairnbawn in the north of
Scotland. This remote site was chosen for security and
because the long sea loch looked like a Norwegian fjord.
Here the submarines and their crews went through
their final and most dangerous exercises.

Simply sailing the tiny subs was tough – like living in a
tiny steel cell. There was no room to stand up or lie
down properly and the air was hot and stale.
Condensation trickled down the hull sides and had to
be endlessly mopped up to stop the delicate electrical
equipment shorting out. But harder still were the
rehearsals for the business end of the mission. Time and
again the crews cut through torpedo nets and lay their
charges under the old battleship *Malaya*.

But would practice make perfect? Now all they had to
do was sneak through the defences protecting the
Tirpitz, place their explosives under her hull and escape
before they exploded.

Easy!

Then There Were Four
The tiny subs had a range of 1,200 miles (1,900 km),
not enough to get them to Altenfjord and back under
their own steam. In the end it was decided to tow

them – with full-size submarines. During the day they would travel submerged, with the midgets coming up briefly every six hours to let in fresh air. Each X-craft was given two crews, one for the sea crossing – the passage crew – and one for the attack – the operational crew. This weird underwater convoy finally got under way at 16:00 on 11 September 1943, each 'tug' and 'tow' setting off at two-hour intervals. The journey across the North Sea, however, was anything but smooth.

X-8

On 15 September, the tow line between *X-8* and the submarine *Sea Nymph* snapped. *X-8* surfaced and bounced around like a cork in rough seas until the *Sea Nymph* finally found her – 36 hours later. By this time the passage crew were worn out and the operational crew had to take over.

But *X-8*'s troubles weren't finished. On 17 September a leak in the starboard buoyancy tank made her unstable, and the only way to correct this was to drop the explosive charges. With no weapons *X-8* was out of the mission and scuttled (deliberately sunk).

One down.

X-9

The tow line between *X-9* and the *Syrtis* parted on 16 September. The *Syrtis* searched all day and most of the night, but *X-9* was never seen again. Her loss has never been explained but it is likely that when the line parted, she took a downward dive. The crew would have had no chance to react and she would have been crushed by the pressure.

Two down.

X-7

On the night of the 19th, with 20 miles to go, *X-7* was on the surface when something bumped against the bow. A drifting German mine had tangled in the tow line! The commander, Lieutenant Godfrey Place, spent seven long minutes untying the broken strands of wire that gripped the mine. Finally he was able to push it clear with his foot, and it floated harmlessly astern.

In the Lair of the Beast

On the evening of Monday 20 September, the submarines gathered off the Norwegian coast. The operational crews took over and the four remaining X-craft dropped their tow ropes. *X-5*, *X-6* and *X-7* were going after the *Tirpitz* and *X-10* the *Scharnhorst*.

That night, under a bright moon, with the northern lights shimmering on the horizon, they tackled the first barrier – the minefields. The Navy had little idea about the type and depth of the mines the Germans had sown, but luckily they had been laid to catch ocean-going ships and submarines. The tiny X-craft, with their shallow drafts, slithered through unscathed.

X-10

At dawn on the 21st mechanical troubles dogged *X-10*.
The periscope motor burned out and filled the craft
with the stench of burning rubber. Lieutenant Hudspeth
put her on the seabed and tried to make repairs. When
these failed she dropped out of the mission and made
her way back to the rendezvous point with the 'tugs'.

Three down.

Now all the remaining subs had the same target – the
Tirpitz.

X-6

X-6, with Lieutenant Donald Cameron in command, was

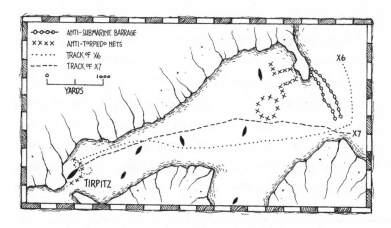

The paths of *X-6* and *X-7* along Kaafford
to the *Tirpitz*.

having problems too – the starboard explosive charge had flooded and she was listing heavily. Even so, on Tuesday 21st she dived and crept slowly up Stern Sound and Altenfjord.

By 04:45 on the 22nd she was at the entrance to Kaafjord. Through his periscope Donald Cameron could see their prey – the *Tirpitz* was barely three miles (4 km) away. But how to get through the submarine nets? Send the diver out to cut them or . . .

Suddenly Donald ordered, 'Stand by to surface. Stand by engine.'

The astonished crew looked at him.

It was daylight.

The sub would be a sitting duck.

Had he gone mad?

And they were nearly right. Donald had just had a really crazy idea.

A trawler was approaching fast and the Germans would have to open the 'gate' in the net to let it through. In a split second he decided to follow the fishing boat in. But to keep up, *X-6* had to surface and use her diesel engine. Amazingly it worked. With the periscope down, and the deck barely above the waves, Donald tucked in behind. Once through the nets into Kaafjord, he yelled, 'Dive, dive, dive,' and the sub slid gratefully into the inky waters.

By 07:00 *X-6* was outside the last barrier, the anti-torpedo nets. But there was a snag, a big one. The periscope had flooded and Donald could hardly see out. Almost blind, the sub edged forward until he noticed some dark blobs on the surface and a gap between them. Guessing the 'blobs' were buoys marking the net and the 'gap' was the boat entrance, he steered for it. When he raised the periscope again the clouded lens was filled with a great grey shape – the *Tirpitz*. *X-6* had reached the target.

But now Donald ran out of luck. At 07:07, as he moved forward to place the charges, the sub hit a rock. The impact was dramatic. *X-6* bounced like an underwater kangaroo – breaking the surface 200 yards (180 m) from the battleship and again only 80 yards (75 m) away. The second time she was spotted by a sailor and the alarm was raised. When Donald surfaced a third time, just off the port beam of the *Tirpitz*, a volley of bullets and grenades rattled off the hull. When he heard the thunk of a German motor launch hitting *X-6* he realized time had run out.

In a flurry the crew released their mines, destroyed mission documents and opened the vents to scuttle the sub. This done, they climbed out of the hatch and surrendered, stepping aboard the enemy boat. Before the Germans could examine the X-craft she sank quietly beneath the waves. The time was 07:25 – the mines were due to go off in less than an hour.

Four down.

Half amused and half horrified, the crew of *X-6* were

taken aboard the *Tirpitz* and locked in a cell for interrogation. Unfortunately there was one thing they couldn't confess.

'Excuse me, old chap, but I regret to inform you there are four tons of explosive under your battleship. Erm . . . possibly twelve if the other X-craft have got through. Can we get off now please?'

If the *Tirpitz* was torn apart they would die in the wreckage.

X-7

X-7 had a good run to the target. Like X-6, she had sneaked through the anti-submarine nets, though not quite as cheekily. Godfrey Place, her commander, waited until a Nazi minesweeper came out of Kaafjord, then slipped in 40 feet (12 m) underwater. But the anti-torpedo nets around the *Tirpitz* were a different story.

At 07:05 X-7 tried to duck under them, submerging to 70 feet (20 m), but was soon tangled in the tight mesh. Urgently Godfrey ran the engines at full pelt and blew the main ballast tanks. When she came loose, he tried again, this time dropping to 90 feet (25 m). Once more he nosed forward and X-7 stuck fast.

'How deep do these confounded things go?' he wondered.

What Godfrey could not know was the *Tirpitz* was protected by two sets of nets. The outer layer stretched down from the surface, while the inner layer rose up from the bottom. On the second dive, X-7 had become trapped in the inner net. When he shook her loose again, the sub surfaced in the gap between them. As Godfrey looked through the periscope he was awestruck to see the *Tirpitz* only 30 yards away.

But this was not the moment to be impressed. He dived immediately and edged down the length of the battleship – until he guessed X-7 was under the bridge.

'Release starboard side charge.'

The first mine fell away, the fuses already set to explode in an hour.

Now the sub ran 200 (60 m) feet astern and dropped the second mine – under the rear gun turrets.

It was 07:20. Time to get away – fast.

Godfrey tried to find the gap in the nets that had let them in – and missed. With the minutes ticking by, he butted hopelessly against the mesh. To add to his troubles, the Germans sighted X-7 and opened fire. Desperately, he surfaced and slid over the top, bullets pinging off the hull – only to collide with another net. Then it was 08:12.

Boom Time

With a dull roar, the mines went off. The *Tirpitz* lifted into the air and crashed back down, listing heavily to port. A large hole was blown in her hull and the rear gun turret was torn loose. The engines were put out of action, together with range finders, radio and radar equipment. Surprisingly, only one sailor was killed, though 40 more were injured. When the Germans completed a damage assessment, they reckoned on six months' work to make the *Tirpitz* fit to go to sea. The X-craft had scored a spectacular hit.

On board the battleship, the crew of *X-6* had mixed emotions. They were disappointed that the *Tirpitz* hadn't sunk, but had to admit it was good to be alive. On board *X-7* the results were dire. The explosion hurled the sub clear of the nets, but caused massive damage. They had little choice but to give up. Yet this was easier said than done. When Godfrey surfaced the Germans opened fire and holed the sub in several places.

X-7 took shelter behind a floating gunnery target and Godfrey leapt out, waving his pullover in surrender. He had barely time to step on to the target before the sub sank. Three men were still inside. Two and a half hours later, Lieutenant Robert Aitken surfaced using an emergency oxygen mask. He was the only one to make it.

Five down.

X-5

X-5, with Lieutenant H. Henty-Creer in command, is the mystery sub of the mission. Godfrey Place saw her on the evening of the 20th, as he steered *X-7* through the minefield. The two skippers signalled 'Good Luck' and 'Good hunting'. Then she wasn't sighted again until the end. About half an hour after the mines went off, *X-5* was spotted 250 yards from the *Tirpitz* and sunk in a hail of fire. There were no survivors. No trace of her has ever been found.

Six down.

FIGHTING FACTS

Mission Accomplished – Almost

Five of the six X-craft were lost and ten crewmen killed. Those captured were held as prisoners until the end of the war. Donald Cameron and Godfrey Place won VCs. The *Tirpitz* had not been sunk, but was so badly damaged that she was unable to move from her anchorage until April 1944.

Eyewitness – Go Ahead, Shoot Him

Edmund Goddard was one of the crew of *X-6*. He was on board the *Tirpitz* when the mines went off. In an BBC interview he retold the events of his capture:

They lined us up before a group of guards with tommy guns; they were all very hostile and murmured Schweinhund *and other things. Then an interpreter came along and asked us about how many boats there were and so on, but we just gave them our names and numbers. He got very annoyed and said if we didn't play, he'd have to shoot us. He pointed at Lorimer and said to me, 'If you don't give the information, I shall shoot your comrade too.' 'Oh well,' I said, 'you go ahead and shoot him.'*

Death of the **Tirpitz**

Since the *Tirpitz* had not been sunk, the Allies kept coming after her. On the night of 10–11 February 1944 Russian bombers attacked with no result.

At dawn on 4 April 1944, the Fleet Air Arm attacked Kaafjord from five British aircraft carriers. Over 60 planes – Barracuda dive-bombers escorted by Corsair, Hellcat and Wildcat fighters – jumped the *Tirpitz* on her first full-speed trials. Repairs from the X-craft raid had just finished. German casualties were heavy – 122 killed and 316 wounded. At least fourteen bombs caused serious damage but the *Tirpitz*'s armoured deck saved her. Three months' gruelling work later, she was ready for action again.

In September 1944 the RAF struck a deal with the Russians. Thirty-six Lancaster bombers from 617 Squadron and 9 Squadron were to be allowed to use a Russian airfield from which to attack the *Tirpitz*. They were equipped with a powerful new weapon – the 21-foot long 'Tallboy' or earthquake bomb, designed by Dr Barnes Wallis.

The Lancasters took off from Yagodnik Island, near Archangel, on 15 September. They sighted the target from 30 miles away, but by the time they were overhead the *Tirpitz* was almost completely hidden by a smoke screen. Only one bomb hit but it blew an enormous hole in the fo'c'sle (the forecastle – near the bow). Two near misses wrecked the armoured deck and engines.

The *Tirpitz* was now so badly damaged that she was moved to Tromso to be used as an artillery battery if the Allies tried to invade Norway. Even though she was no longer a threat at sea the RAF came again. At 09:40 on 12 November, a three minute attack dropped two 'Tallboys' on to the battleship and two ships next to her. The great ship was ripped open like a tin can and slowly turned turtle. The story of the *Tirpitz* was finally over.

GLOSSARY

Barrage balloons – massive helium balloons held in place
by steel cables. With luck enemy planes would get
caught in the cables and crash

Corvette – cheap convoy escort ship

Fleigerkorps – German air army

Hydroplane – a flat fin for controlling the upward and
downward movements of the submarine

Kriegsmarine – German navy

Morale – will to carry on (fighting), general spirits

Oerlikon cannon – a 20mm quick-firing gun designed in
Sweden

Pocket battleship – small battleship

ACKNOWLEDGEMENTS

Imperial War Museum: p.9 2222575H, p.38 HU832610, p.39 A4161, p.43 HU374, p.50 HU400, p.64 C2647, p.65 A17826, p.68 HU63112, p.75 MH24176, p.99 A19625; Robert Hunt Library: p.27 O1825, p.32 A18276; Hulton Getty: p.46 KEY905737(AX).

Special thanks to: John Wellham for his kind assistance with Operation Judgement. It was daunting to write a story knowing he was checking it! Mrs Brewin for permission to use her husband's account in 'The Bloody Beaches of Dieppe'.

Also, grateful acknowledgement is made to the Imperial War Museum for permission to use Jack Brewin's account of his time at Dieppe.

Every effort has been made to trace copyright holders. We would be grateful to hear from any copyright holders not acknowledged here.

A WORLD IN FLAMES
CIVILIANS

Neil Tonge

Six fantastic stories about civilians during World War II.

In 1939 three and a half million children are evacuated from towns and cities that are likely to be bombed. What will Judy's new life in Lydney be like?

By July 1940 nearly half a million applications have been made for children to be evacuated overseas. What will happen to the children on the ship *The City of Benares*, heading for Canada, which is torpedoed by a German U-boat?

In 1939 there are seventy thousand Germans and Austrians living in Britain. What will become of them when war is declared?

The German army overruns France in six weeks in 1940! How are the French Resistance going to disrupt the occupation of France?

In October 1940 Coventry is devastated by an air-raid by the German air force. How do the people of Coventry react?

Packed with fighting facts and black and white photographs.

A WORLD IN FLAMES
WAR IN THE AIR

Peter Hepplewhite

Six fantastic stories about war in the air during World War II.

In 1940 Stuka dive-bombers pound a Sussex radar station. Will they knock out Britain's warning systems and pave the way for a German invasion?

As the Battle of Britain reaches its height a desperate Hurricane pilot runs out of ammunition. How can he stop a German bomber heading straight for Buckingham Palace?

Deadly Focke-Wulf fighters pounce on a Lancaster bomber over Berlin. Does the stricken plane stand a chance of ever making it home?

Trapped by searing anti-aircraft fire, an American B-17 bomber bursts in flames. Will the courage of one crewman be enough to fight the fire?

Blowing down the walls of Amiens prison to rescue 700 Resistance fighters. Is this a mission impossible for the Mosquito squadrons?

During the summer of 1944 a new weapon blasts London. Can Britain's best fighter pilots stop the sinister V1 flying bombs?

Packed with fighting facts and black and white photographs.